Sherborne Abbey Cookbook

Line drawings and design by Peter Haillay

Sherborne Abbey Cookbook

A book of traditional recipes
produced in aid of the Sherborne Abbey Appeal

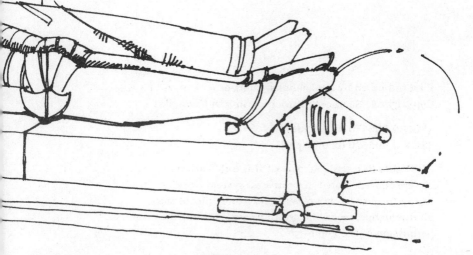

Alphabooks

Favourite and original recipes contributed by the people and friends of Sherborne to help the Appeal for the restoration of Sherborne Abbey.

First published by Alphabooks, Sherborne, Dorset in 1979
Copyright © Sherborne Parochial Church Council

ISBN 0 906670 01 2 (cloth)
ISBN 0 906670 02 0 (paper)

Printed by T. J. Press (Padstow) Ltd, Padstow, Cornwall.

CONTENTS

ACKNOWLEDGMENTS

Thank you for buying this book and thereby helping the Sherborne Abbey Appeal, which will receive all the profits from sale.

We also thank the many people who have contributed recipes, not least those whose recipes have had to be left out through lack of space. The numbers and types of recipes received have helped us to decide what sort of dishes would prove to be the most popular.

We are very grateful to the shopkeepers of Sherborne who helped to gather in the recipes for us, the marvellous band of typists, our publishers for their very generous help and support, and finally our families and friends who put up with endless piles of paper over every available surface when we were compiling the book, bread and cheese lunches half an hour late when we were busy sorting and writing, and added inches when we were testing. Thank you all.

Christine Stones
Pat Appleyard
Joan Miller

SHERBORNE ABBEY

Sherborne Abbey has justly been described as one of the most beautiful churches in Europe. Dignified and gracious, glowing warm with golden Ham Stone, the exterior is mostly fifteenth century. Inside, the nave and chancel with their magnificently vaulted roofs are linked by the soaring eleventh-century Norman arches which support the tower, and the heaviest peal of eight bells in the world. Side chapels of different centuries grace the building; at the east is the restored Lady Chapel, with its modern engraved glass reredos. The story of the Abbey covers 1250 years, Cathedral of Wessex from 705 to 1075, the heart of a Benedictine Abbey until 1539, and parish church of St Mary the Virgin for the last 400 years.

In 1975 the superb fan vaulting of the Abbey was found to be in danger, owing to the poor condition of the lead covering the roofs which had been laid some 150 years before. A major Appeal was therefore launched in May 1977, with a target of £200,000. Since then the work has gone ahead, not only renewing the lead covering the roofs, but in repairing the roof timbers found to be rotting beneath, replacing damaged stonework, and renewing lead work in clerestory windows − much more than was originally planned, but all thought vital if this great building is to be protected for future generations.

THE ABBEY

I put my helmet on,
And climbed up a ladder so long,
I climbed up another, another and another,
Up so high,
Up in the sky.

I climbed another, so little that one was
and there I was touching the Abbey roof
for ever,
So down we went,
For ever never stopping,
So high in the sky we were yesterday,
On the Abbey roof.

Lucinda Harvey,   age 9

Soups

ICED BEETROOT SOUP

4 large cooked beets
2 pints aspic jelly
¼ pint vinegar
　　salt and pepper

Serves 8

1. Grate the beetroot into the aspic jelly.
2. Add the vinegar and seasoning and leave to set.

Mrs Jean Griffiths

HARVEST MOON SOUP

1 pint plain yoghurt
1 pint tomato juice
　　pinch oregano
6 oz peeled prawns (optional)

1 teaspoon lemon juice
½ cucumber
1 tablespoon grated onion

Serves 6

1. Combine the yoghurt, tomato juice, oregano and lemon juice.
2. Peel, chop and deseed the cucumber. Salt and drain.
3. Add the prawns, cucumber and onion to the soup.
4. Mix well.
5. Serve chilled.

Mrs Jane Privett

ICED YOGHURT SOUP

½ pint yoghurt
¼ pint double cream
1 large cucumber
½ pint shrimps or prawns
   salt, pepper, garlic and a handful of fresh mint

Serves 4

1. Mix yoghurt and cream well together.
2. Peel cucumber and grate coarsely or cut into slivers before stirring into yoghurt.
3. Add prawns, salt, pepper and garlic to taste. Chill thoroughly. Before serving remove garlic and stir in chopped mint.

Mrs Pip Rogers

CHRISTINA'S GAZPACHO

1 large tin tomatoes
¼ cucumber
½ green pepper
½ red pepper

1 slice of bread
1 clove garlic
2 tablespoons white wine
  vinegar
2 tablespoons olive oil
  salt and pepper

Serves 6

1. Blend all the ingredients together.
2. Chill.
3. Consume.

Mrs Jane Privett

COLD CREAMED ORANGE AND CARROT SOUP

1 lb new carrots
1 onion
1 oz butter
1½ pints chicken stock
  salt

1 level teaspoon sugar
  juice of 4 oranges
¼ pint single cream
  chopped chives

Serves 6

1. Scrape the carrots and slice thinly.
2. Melt the butter in a saucepan and add the peeled and thinly sliced, carrots and onion. Fry gently for a few minutes to soften the vegetables but do not brown them.
3. Stir in the stock, salt and sugar, bring to the boil, cover with a lid and simmer gently for one hour.
4. Draw the pan off the heat and pass the soup through a sieve or purée in a liquidiser.
5. Add the strained juice of the oranges and then the cream.
6. Heat until thoroughly mixed, then chill for several hours. Sprinkle with chopped chives and serve.

Mrs M. Truett

SOUPE A LA BONNE FEMME (Leek and Potato soup)

4—6 medium leeks, peeled and
sliced
3—4 medium potatoes, peeled
and diced
2—3 oz butter
1 pint or more of good stock

1 pint milk
salt
freshly ground black pepper
cream

Serves 8

1. Put the leeks and potatoes with the butter into a thick pan and cook very slowly over a gentle heat for about 15 minutes.
2. Add stock to cover and simmer gently until the potatoes are cooked.
3. Put the soup through a liquidiser or sieve.
4. Add the milk, reheat but do not boil.
5. Add sufficient salt to flavour, and pepper to taste. This soup may be served very hot or very cold. In either case, stir in a little cream before serving.

Kettner maintained that _soupe à la bonne femme_ was an attempt to paint the character of a good woman; a culinary portrait uniting two principle concepts of womanhood symbolised in the malleability of cream and the acidity of sorrel. In the course of repeated reproductions of the good lady's portrait, _la bonne femme_ has lost some of the clarity of the original. This is the soup in its better known form using leeks instead of the sorrel.

Mrs Katherine Barker

CREAM OF WATERCRESS SOUP

2 bunches watercress
2 oz finely chopped onion
1 oz butter
1½ pints milk

1 oz flour
2 egg yolks
2 tablespoons cream
bunch of bacon rinds tied
together

Serves 6

1. Chop the watercress.
2. Melt the butter and add the watercress and onion. Cover and cook gently for 8 minutes.
3. Add the flour and gradually stir in the milk.
4. Season well, add the bacon rinds, cover and simmer for 20 minutes.
5. Remove the rinds and either sieve the soup or put it in a liquidiser.
6. Add the yolks beaten in the cream.
7. Reheat without boiling when required and serve with fried croûtons.

This soup is very nice served cold in the summer.

Mrs Sheila Samuel

BROAD BEAN SOUP

1 lb broad beans
1 pint stock
   savory or thyme

1 teaspoon arrowroot
¼ pint milk or cream
1 oz butter
   seasoning

Serves 4

1. Cook the beans in the stock with herbs for 20 minutes.
2. Rub through a sieve or liquidise.
3. Mix the arrowroot with milk or cream and add to the purée.
4. Simmer for a few minutes and then add the butter.

This is useful for tough beans left on the plant too long!

Mrs Jean Griffiths

TURNIP SOUP

3—4 lb white turnip
2 oz onion
2 pints stock
1½ oz butter

1½ oz flour
2—3 egg yolks
2—3 tablespoons cream
 salt and pepper

Serves 8

1. Melt the butter, add the flour and cook for 2 minutes.
2. Add the stock and vegetables stirring well, and simmer for 40 minutes.
3. Sieve or liquidise.
4. Mix the yolks and cream and thicken over a bain-marie, and then add to the soup.
5. Adjust seasoning.

This soup can easily be served without being thickened, but perhaps add a little cream just before serving.

Mrs Jean Griffiths

COURGETTE SOUP

1½ lb courgettes
½ oz butter
1 tablespoon oil
1 tablespoon chopped parsley

1¾ pints chicken stock
2 eggs
1 oz grated cheese

Serves 6

1. Wash and dice the unpeeled courgettes.
2. Melt the butter with oil and brown the courgettes.
3. Add the stock, bring to the boil and simmer until the courgettes are soft.
4. Liquidise or pass through a fine sieve and return to the pan.
5. Beat the eggs, cheese and herbs together in a bowl.
6. Add a ladleful of hot soup to the egg mixture, stir, and pour it gradually into the rest of the soup stirring over a low heat. Do not allow to boil. Season to taste.

Mrs Philippa Sherwin

JERUSALEM ARTICHOKE SOUP

1½ lb artichokes
½ lb potatoes
1½ teaspoons lemon juice

2 pints good chicken or beef
  stock
  salt and black pepper
1 egg yolk
4 tablespoons cream

Serves 8

1. Peel and cook the artichokes and potatoes in the stock.
2. Add the lemon juice — then rub through a fine sieve or purée in a liquidiser.
3. Add salt and pepper and bring to the boil. Reduce the heat and add the well-beaten egg yolk and cream just before serving.

This soup freezes well, but do not add the egg yolk and cream until just before serving.

Mrs Windham

PRAWN AND CORN CHOWDER

1 large onion, finely chopped
½ oz butter
½ pint stock
1 lb potatoes, diced
  salt and pepper

4 oz prawns
7 oz tin sweetcorn, drained
¾ pint milk
3 oz grated cheese

Serves 4

1. Lightly fry the onion in butter until soft but not coloured.
2. Add the stock, potatoes and seasoning. Bring to the boil.
3. Cover, simmer gently for 10—15 minutes until the potatoes are just cooked.
4. Liquidise.
5. Add the prawns, sweetcorn and milk and reheat.
6. Take off the heat and stir in the cheese.

Mrs Diana Duff

PSAROSOUPA ME AVGOLEMONO
(Fish soup with Egg and Lemon sauce)

2 lb white fish	salt and pepper
2 large onions	
6 pints water	*Egg and lemon sauce*
½ cup olive oil	juice of one lemon
4 celery stalks with leaves	2 eggs
3 carrots	

Serves 10

1. Clean and then cut the fish into pieces, not too small. Rub with salt and lemon.
2. Clean the vegetables and cut these into chunky pieces but even so not too large.
3. Put the water into a pan and bring it smartly to the boil, then add the oil, stir this well, and when it is blended, add the vegetables, reduce the heat and cook steadily for 40 minutes. Reduce the heat to simmering, add the pieces of fish and cook carefully for 20 minutes. The fish should not break, so cooking must be very slow.
4. When the fish is tender, take it from the pan, put it aside but keep hot.
5. Strain the stock and vegetables through a sieve and return to the pan. Reheat the strained fish stock, add the egg and lemon sauce (see below), stir it well into the soup (not allowing it to boil) and then pour the soup over the fish.

Some Greek cooks add rice to this type of soup which makes, of course, a more substantial dish. To the above quantity of soup, add 3 oz of long grain rice after the fish has been removed and the soup strained. Cook it only just long enough to make the rice tender, then add the sauce and continue as above.

Egg and lemon sauce
Beat the 2 eggs until fluffy and light, then slowly add the lemon juice, beating all the while. Gradually add 2 or 3 tablespoons of the stock from the dish you are making. Leave for 5 minutes on the side of the stove — above all, do not let the sauce boil, and keep the pan covered.

Mrs Dina Bailey

SUMMER SOUP

2 lettuce leaves	salt and pepper
a few leaves of watercress	2 egg yolks
a few leaves of tarragon	2 tablespoons milk
¼ cucumber	1 tablespoon cream
1 pint white stock	

Serves 4

1. Shred the vegetables finely and toss them in the butter until it is absorbed.
2. Add the boiling stock and cook for a few minutes.
3. Add half the milk.
4. Mix egg yolks, cream and remaining milk together; strain into the soup and thicken without boiling until the yolks are cooked.

Mrs H. T. B. Mimpriss

CREAM OF CUCUMBER SOUP

3 young cucumbers
2 oz butter
  pinch of sugar
  salt and freshly milled pepper
1 pint stock (chicken stock cube)
¼ pint single cream
  few extra cucumber slices to garnish

White sauce
½ pint milk
½ onion
1 bay leaf
1 oz butter
1 oz plain flour

Serves 4

1. Make the white sauce. Put the milk, onion and bay leaf on to boil, then draw the pan off the heat and leave to infuse for 10 minutes.
2. Melt the butter in a small saucepan and stir in flour. Cook for 2 minutes.
3. Stir in the strained milk and bring to the boil stirring well. Cook gently for 2—3 minutes. Set aside.
4. Peel the cucumbers, slice in half lengthwise, remove the seeds and slice the flesh thinly.
5. Blanch in boiling water for 2 minutes, then drain.
6. Melt the butter in a heavy pan — add the cucumber, sugar, salt and pepper.
7. Cover and cook gently until soft (approximately 15 minutes).
8. Add the chicken stock and prepared white sauce.
9. Liquidise and then return the soup to the saucepan to reheat. Stir in the cream just before serving. Garnish with a few thinly cut blanched slices of cucumber.

Mrs Alison Underwood

SHERBORNE ABBEY

Caged in by scaffolding,
Stands the Abbey.
Its roof rotting.
Slates are replaced,
Stones taken out.
The scaffolding covers up
The beautiful carvings
And delicate windows.
Help pay for slates and stones,
Help repair the Abbey,
So the rotting and decaying,
Can be forgotten.

Rachel Carter   *age 11*

First Courses

COQUILLES ST JACQUES A LA CURE

8 fresh scallops or 1 lb frozen scallops
seasoning
1 pint white sauce with garlic and parsley
¼ lb grated cheese
glass of white wine

Serves 8

1. Make a thick, well-seasoned white sauce with the wine. If you like garlic, garlic granules improve this dish.
2. When you are happy with the sauce, add the scallops chopped into quarters, together with any juice. Cook well. There is a slight tendency to undercook scallops, and the flavour is not released. Taste the sauce and this will indicate when the scallops are cooked.
3. Place in shallow ramekin dishes or egg dishes. Cover with grated cheese and grill until bubbly and brown. Then sit down and enjoy it!

Paul Goddard
Vicar of Sherborne

PRAWNS IN TOMATO

2 tins condensed tomato soup
1 small tin red peppers
1 hard-boiled egg

1 medium onion
¼ lb mushrooms
8 oz prawns

Serves 4

1. Put the soup into a double saucepan. Finely chop the onion and fry in butter until soft. Add to the soup.
2. Add the chopped red peppers without juice and sliced mushrooms, and finely chopped hard-boiled egg to the soup and onions.
3. Heat gently and add the prawns. Season to taste. Serve with long grain rice (2 oz per person).

Quick and easy.

Mrs D. Saunders

SALMON CRUMBLE

Crumble mixture
6 oz white breadcrumbs
3 oz butter
  salt and pepper

Salmon filling

1 medium tin salmon	1 oz butter
1 oz flour	½ pint milk
juice of ½ a lemon	1 egg yolk
¼ peeled cucumber	seasoning

Serves 6

1. Fry the breadcrumbs gently in butter until golden brown and season lightly.
2. Drain and flake the salmon.
3. Make a basic white sauce with the butter, flour and milk, remove from the heat, add the lemon juice and beat in the egg yolk.
4. Add the salmon and heat for 2 minutes without boiling, add the diced cucumber and seasoning.
5. Arrange layers of salmon and breadcrumbs alternately in a heated dish, finishing with a layer of breadcrumbs.
6. Bake for 15 minutes in a 375-400°F., Gas No. 5-6 oven. Serve with thin slices of brown bread and butter.

Mrs Mollie Carr

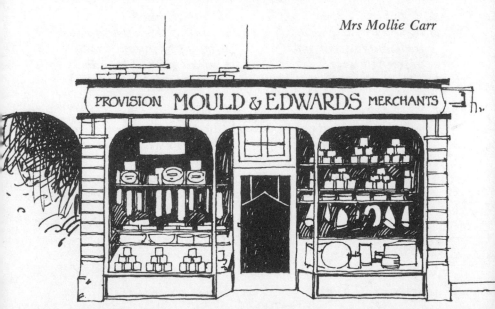

STILTON PATE

1 oz butter
¼—½ pint milk
  cayenne pepper
4 stuffed olives, chopped
4 oz Blue Stilton, grated

1 oz flour
salt and pepper
1 level tablespoon mayonnaise
1 clove garlic, crushed

Serves 4

1. Melt the butter in a saucepan, stir in the flour and cook for 1—2 minutes.
2. Gradually blend in the milk.
3. Return to the heat and bring to the boil stirring constantly.
4. Cool completely.
5. Add the mayonnaise, olives, garlic, cheese and seasoning to taste, and mix thoroughly. (For a very smooth pâté this can all be done in the liquidiser.)
6. Place in 4 individual dishes or 1 large dish and chill until required.
7. Garnish the pâté with an extra sliced stuffed olive and serve with hot toast and butter.

Mrs M. E. Bradley

LARGE ECONOMICAL PATE OR TERRINE

¾ lb pig or ox liver
¾ lb sausage meat
  garlic, herbs, salt and
  pepper to taste

¾ lb beef mince
¾ pint of thick white sauce
1 chopped onion, fried
1 small glass of brandy
  (optional, but good)

Serves a lot

1. Fry the liver and put it through the mincer.
2. Mix the rest of the ingredients in a large bowl really thoroughly.
3. Put into a big bread tin or pâté dish.
4. Cover with either tin foil or a lid. Place in a meat dish half filled with water and bake at 375°F., Gas No. 5 for an hour.

Mrs Mary Goddard

LUXURY KIPPER PATE

8–9 small boneless kipper
  fillets
  juice of 1 lemon

¼ pint single cream
2 teaspoons Camp coffee
  pepper

Serves 6

1. Grill the kippers flat side uppermost for 3½–4 minutes under a moderate grill.
2. Skin, removing all the flesh.
3. Liquidise with cream, lemon juice, coffee and freshly ground black pepper until smooth. Serve with lemon and toast.

Mrs J. Austin

ELNA'S EASY PARTY PATE

¼ lb liver sausage
1 teaspoon curry powder
1 tablespoon sherry
  nut of butter

¼ lb Demi-sel or sieved cottage
  cheese
1 tablespoon Worcester sauce

Serves 6

Blend all the ingredients together and serve with toast.

Mrs E. Kemp

TUNA FISH DELIGHT

1 tin condensed mushroom soup
8 oz tin tuna fish
  golden breadcrumbs

Serves 6

1. Drain oil from tuna fish and mix with soup.
2. Turn into ramekin dishes.
3. Sprinkle with breadcrumbs.
4. Put into preheated oven at 350°F., Gas No. 4 for 15 minutes.
5. Serve with brown bread and butter.

Mrs E. Penrose

25

TARAMASALATA

6 oz smoked cod's roe
¼ Spanish onion, finely
  grated
6—8 tablespoons olive oil

6 slices white bread
1 clove garlic, chopped (optional)
juice of ½ a lemon

Serves 6

1. Place the cod's roe in a mortar.
2. Trim the crusts from the bread and make into breadcrumbs.
3. Dampen slightly and add to the roe and pound to a smooth paste.
4. Stir in the onion and the garlic.
5. Add the oil and lemon juice little by little.
6. Stir well and season.

Chill before serving this delicious Greek pâté.

Mrs Pip Rogers

CHICKEN LIVER PATE

4 chicken livers
1 oz butter
1 sliced green pepper (or
  parsley)
  a little melted butter

4 rashers of streaky bacon
1 clove garlic
1 cup top of the milk
1 egg

Serves 6

1. Cook the livers and bacon in the butter until the liver is soft.
2. Place in the liquidiser with the garlic, pepper and top of the milk and blend until smooth.
3. Place in dishes and cook for 25—35 minutes in a moderate oven (350°F., Gas No. 4) standing in dish of water.
4. When cooked, pour the melted butter on top and put the paté in the fridge.

George Reindorp
The Lord Bishop of Salisbury

WALDORF APPLES

For each person:

1 rosy dessert apple	½ oz shelled walnuts
½ stick celery	1 dessertspoon mayonnaise
celery top for garnish	

1. Take the stalk off the apple, remove the top and core. Scoop out the centre with a small spoon.
2. Blend the chopped apple, celery and walnuts and add the mayonnaise.
3. Fill the centre of the apple and garnish with the celery top.

Try adding small cubes of Stilton cheese to the other ingredients in the apple for a tasty extra.

Mrs E. Corbridge

HOT EGG AND PRAWN RAMEKINS

4 hard-boiled eggs	1 tablespoon French mustard
1 tablespoon breadcrumbs	1 small tin prawns
¼ pint double cream	1 oz butter
2 tablespoons freshly chopped parsley	1 tablespoon grated cheese
	salt and pepper

Serves 4

1. Chop the eggs finely, and mix lightly together with the prawns, mustard, salt and pepper, parsley and cream.
2. Put into small fireproof ramekins and sprinkle with the mixed grated cheese and breadcrumbs.
3. Dot with small pieces of butter. Put into a moderate oven (350°F., Gas No. 4) for 10-15 minutes until hot and brown on top. Serve immediately.

Mrs Julia Wallen

2 tins of sweet corn (approximately 12 oz size)
½ pint homemade mayonnaise (if possible)
½ pint cream, whipped stiffly
2 chopped hard-boiled eggs
curry powder

Serves 8

1. Season the whipped cream.
2. Drain the sweetcorn well, and fold into the cream.
3. Sprinkle the finely chopped hard-boiled eggs on top.
4. Season the mayonnaise with curry powder to taste and spread liberally on top.
5. Serve with slices of thin brown bread and butter.

This is best served in a large, shallow dish, the cream must not be too 'flimsy' otherwise it collapses to the bottom. Should you have two more to feed, add a small tin of sweetcorn.

CUCUMBER MOUSSE

¼ lb Philadelphia cream cheese
1 packet (½ oz) gelatine
¼ pint chicken stock
1 desertspoon lemon juice
¼ pint cream, sour cream or yoghurt
1 cucumber
salt and black pepper

Serves 4

1. Beat together the cream cheese and the cream, sour cream or yoghurt until smooth. (Use cream for a richer dish, yoghurt for a simple unfattening one.)
2. Melt the gelatine in the stock, grate the peeled cucumber and mix it into the cheese mixture.
3. Add the lemon juice, salt and black pepper to taste.
4. Pour the heated gelatine through a strainer into the mixture and stir thoroughly. When well mixed, pour into a soufflé dish or mould and chill.

Miss Ruth Stocker

STUFFED MUSHROOMS

1½ tablespoons sliced onions   *1 tablespoon butter*
¼ cup soft breadcrumbs   *¼ cup chopped walnuts*
1½ tablespoons chilli sauce   *1½ tablespoons lemon juice*
    pepper to taste   *1 lb large mushrooms*

Serves 6—8

1. Sauté mushrooms in butter.
2. Mix together all the other ingredients.
3. Place the mixture in the mushrooms and heat under the grill, and serve hot.

STUFFED ARTICHOKE BOTTOMS

4 cooked fresh artichoke
bottoms (tinned will do
if necessary)
lettuce, cress, seasoning
and a little mayonnaise

1 small tin tuna fish
2 hard-boiled eggs
8 anchovy fillets

Serves 4

1. Drain the cooked artichoke bottoms and arrange on a bed of crisp lettuce.
2. Mix the drained tuna fish with a little mayonnaise and season to taste.
3. Fill the artichokes with this mixture. Place half a hard-boiled egg, dome side up, on the tuna fish, then arrange 2 anchovy fillets crosswise on top. Add a dash of paprika.
4. Sprinkle a little cress around the artichoke and serve with a salad dressing.

Having had this while on holiday in France, we have experimented until we found out how to prepare it exactly the same.

Mrs Chris Tanner

AVOCADO (OR PEAR) AND APPLE

2 avocados, or 4 dessert
pears
1 lettuce
4–6 oz grated cheese
lemon juice

4 small eating apples
4 tomatoes
small cucumber
French dressing
paprika

Serves 4

1. Shred the lettuce, chop the tomatoes, cucumber, pears and apples and mix together, giving a squeeze of lemon juice to prevent discoloration.
2. Place on bed of lettuce on small plates; spoon over French dressing and sprinkle with grated cheese and paprika.

Mrs Julia Perry

TOMATO ICE CREAM

2 separated eggs
¼ pint double cream
8 drops Worcester sauce

1 oz icing sugar
3 dessertspoons tomato
concentrate

1½ pint plastic container

Serves 6

1. Whisk the egg yolks lightly with a fork.
2. Whisk the egg whites to stiff peaks, beat in the sifted icing sugar a little at a time.
3. Slowly beat in the egg yolks.
4. Lightly whip the cream, fold it into the egg mixture, add the tomato concentrate and Worcester sauce and mix thoroughly.
5. Freeze in the container for at least 2 hours.

Serve in sundae dishes suitably garnished with watercress, lettuce or cucumber.

BAKED AVOCADOS WITH CRAB

1 oz butter
4—5 oz crab meat
1—3 tablespoons cream
salt and pepper
2 ripe avocados
parsley

1 small chopped onion
3 tablespoons fresh breadcrumbs
paprika
½ cup Emmenthal or Cheddar
cheese

Serves 4

1. Fry the onion in butter. Add the crab meat and cook for 3—4 minutes.
2. Stir in the breadcrumbs and cream, season with salt, pepper and paprika.
3. Halve the avocados and remove the stones. Put in a baking dish, spoon on the mixture, sprinkle on grated cheese and bake at 350°F., Gas No. 4 for 15—20 minutes.

Mrs Jeni Atherton

GRAPEFRUIT AND AVOCADO SALAD

4 oz cream cheese
1 avocado pear
lettuce

2 grapefruit
French dressing
paprika

Serves 4

1. Shape the cheese into balls, dust with paprika and chill.
2. Peel the grapefruit, removing the skin and the membrane. Remove the sections with a sharp knife.
3. Cut the avocado into quarters lengthwise and pull off the skin. Slice.
4. Arrange fanwise, grapefruit and avocado alternately on the lettuce leaves. Pour over French dressing to which any spilt grapefruit juice is added.
5. Place the cheese balls at the centre of the fan. This savoury can be served in either individual salad dishes, or on a single large bowl.

Mrs B. Morton

AUBERGINES PROVENCALES

2 large aubergines
1 medium onion
4 tomatoes
1 clove garlic
parsley, thyme, basil
1 oz grated cheese
absorbent kitchen paper

salt
1 small green pepper
2 tablespoons oil
2 hard-boiled eggs
1 oz breadcrumbs
black pepper

Serves 4

1. Cut the aubergines in half lengthwise, then cut round the inside and criss-cross the surfaces. Sprinkle with salt and leave for 15 minutes.
2. Peel and slice the onion finely, and cook in oil until tender and golden.

3. Deseed the green pepper and slice finely. Keep four circles, chop the rest and add to the onions.
4. Turn the aubergines on to paper to drain. Scoop out the insides carefully, and add to the onions and green pepper. Cook gently. Add finely crushed garlic.
5. Peel the tomatoes. Keep four slices, chop the rest and add to the mixture.
6. Season with herbs and pepper.
7. Half fill each aubergine case with the mixture. Slice the hard-boiled eggs and lay on top. Then cover with the rest of the mixture, and sprinkle all over with breadcrumbs and grated cheese.
8. Bake in a hot oven (400°F., Gas No. 6) for 20 minutes. Put on the decorative rings of green pepper and tomato 10 minutes before serving.

This is a fairly substantial first course and also makes an excellent light supper dish.

Mrs Julia Wallen

AVOCADO WITH A DIFFERENCE

2 avocados
½ teaspoon salt
  pepper to taste
1 tablespoon lemon juice

¼ pint double or whipping
  cream
2 cloves garlic, crushed
  dash of Worcester sauce

Serves 4

1. Whip the cream with the salt, pepper, garlic, lemon juice and Worcester sauce until stiff.
2. Taste and adjust seasoning remembering that there must be plenty of garlic.
3. Just before serving fill the halved and stoned avocados with cream. Garnish with lemon slices.

Mrs Francis Moule

33

CREAMED EGGS

8 hard-boiled eggs
¼ pint cream
  seasoning and chives

1 tin Crosse & Blackwell
  consommé

Serves 6

1. Blend the yolks of the eggs with the consommé.
2. Add salt, pepper, paprika and Worcester sauce to taste. Place in fridge to set.
3. Chop egg whites, add the salt, whipped cream and chopped chives and mix. (This should be of rice pudding consistency.)
4. Spread the egg-white mixture on top of the yolks and consommé when set. Serve with thin brown bread and butter or Melba toast.

Mrs Jo Binney

DANISH BLUE SAVOURY

½ oz gelatine
4 oz Danish Blue cheese
2–4 oz chopped walnuts
2 tablespoons tomato
  ketchup

4 tablespoons water
¼ pint double cream
2 eggs, separated
  lettuce, black grapes and
  walnuts to decorate

Serves 4–6

1. Dissolve the gelatine in water over a gentle heat, stirring continuously. Cool.
2. Finely grate or mash the cheese.
3. Whisk the cream until fairly stiff.
4. Mix the cheese, tomato ketchup, egg yolks and walnuts together.
5. Whisk the egg whites until stiff, add cool gelatine to the cheese mixture and gently fold in the egg whites. Pour into a well-greased mould and leave in a cool place to set.
6. Turn out just before serving—decorate with lettuce, grapes and walnuts.

GRAPEFRUIT AND WALNUT SALAD

1 large grapefruit, cut in half
3 tablespoons soured cream
1 small onion, chopped finely
2 oz roughly chopped walnut
  halves

12 oz cream cheese or cottage
  cheese
1 tablespoon lemon juice
  salt and pepper
  a little lettuce to garnish

Serves 5—6

1. Remove the grapefruit segments.
2. Mix together the cream or cottage cheese, soured cream, chopped onion, salt, pepper and lemon juice.
3. Add the grapefruit segments and chopped walnuts, and stir in lightly.
4. Serve in individual small glass bowls on a bed of finely shredded lettuce.

An attractive, light starter for a summer meal.

Mrs Julia Wallen

CONSOMME CASTLES

2 level teaspoons gelatine
1 10½ oz tin beef con-
  sommé
4 oz cold cooked peas
  garnish: watercress and
  sliced tomato

¼ pint boiling water
1 tablespoon sherry
2 oz sliced tongue cut into
  small squares

Serves 6

1. Dissolve the gelatine in the boiling water and add the soup and sherry.
2. Chill until almost set, then fold in the tongue and half the peas.
3. Spoon into individual moulds, and allow to set.
4. Turn out and garnish with watercress, tomato and remaining peas.

Mrs K. Vallance

JING DUN STEAMED EGGS

2 eggs, beaten
1 teaspoon vegetable oil
¼ pint water
   few chopped chives

2 teaspoons dry sherry
   pinch salt, pepper and sugar
1 tablespoon Soy sauce (or
   Maggi)

Serves 2

1. Stir all the ingredients into the beaten eggs.
2. Steam in 2 greased bowls or ramekins in the oven at 300°F.,
   Gas No. 2 for about 10 minutes in a bain-marie or until firm.
3. Serve with thin toast, and a little Soy sauce on top (optional).

Mrs Barbara Mallows

BEEF CONSOMME MOUSSE

2 tins beef consommé
12 oz cream cheese
1 level dessertspoon curry powder

Serves 6

1. Whisk the ingredients until smooth either by hand or in a
   liquidiser.
2. Chill the mixture for several hours.
3. Serve garnished with a little caviar (use caviar-style lumpfish
   roe) or with chopped chives or parsley.

Lord Harding of Petherton

Main Courses

TROUT WITH ALMOND SAUCE

2 trout
1 tablespoon ground almonds
1 teaspoon lemon juice
salt and pepper

2 tablespoons butter
½ tablespoon Parmesan cheese
½ teaspoon sugar

Serves 2

1. Gut the trout, leaving on the head, rinse and pat dry. Grill with a brushing of oil, for 6—8 minutes on one side and only half grill the other.
2. Melt 2 tablespoons of butter, add the ground almonds, Parmesan cheese, sugar, lemon juice and salt and pepper to taste.
3. Simmer gently until the sauce is made. It should be 'pasty' enough to stick to the fish and not run off.
4. Now paint the sauce on the half-grilled side of the fish and grill until the sauce is crisp. If there is any sauce left, pour it over the fish before serving.

Jock Henderson

HEREFORD CHICKEN

3½ lb chicken, jointed
1 dessertspoon curry
powder

2 onions
¾ pint cider

Serves 6

1. Brown the floured joints in 2 tablespoons of oil.
2. Cook the onions and curry powder in cider.
3. Place all the ingredients in a casserole and cook in a moderate oven (350°F., Gas No. 4) for 1 hour.

This is improved by adding 2 tablespoons cream just before serving. Decorate with pineapple rings or pieces.

Mrs Jean Wood

SPICED SPATCHCOCK CHICKEN

3½ lb chicken
¼ teaspoon whole cumin
   seeds
½ inch green ginger root,
   grated
1½—2 teaspoons sea salt
   grated rind of ½ lemon

2 oz butter
2 teaspoons whole coriander
4 whole cardamoms, shelled
½ teaspoon ground black
   pepper
1 clove garlic, crushed

Sauce

1 onion, finely chopped
1 teaspoon turmeric
1 tablespoon currants
¼ teaspoon cornflour
4 tablespoons milk

2 oz butter
1 tablespoon ground almonds
2 tablespoons yoghurt
2 tablespoons cream

Serves 6

1. Pound all the whole spices in a mortar until finely powdered.
2. Cream the butter and add spices, salt, garlic and lemon.
3. Slip your fingers between the skin and flesh of the chicken breast to loosen, also loosen skin from the chicken legs.
4. Pack the spiced butter over the chicken breast and legs under the skin.
5. Cut the chicken down the back from neck to tail, snip through the wishbone and press the chicken out flat.
6. Leave to marinate for 1—2 hours then roast in a hot oven (425°F., Gas No. 7) for 35—45 minutes, basting after 15 and 25 minutes with the prepared sauce. Serve with plain boiled rice over which you spoon the buttery roasting juices.

Sauce

1. Melt the butter and gently fry the onion until golden brown.
2. Add turmeric, almonds and currants and fry for 1—2 minutes, then moisten with the combined yoghurt, cornflour, cream and milk.
3. Simmer down a little and spoon over the roasting chicken in two lots.

Nicola Cox

CHICKEN CLEMENTINE

1 large chicken
1 bouquet garni
2 oz butter
1 pint stock
2 egg yolks

1 bay leaf
1 sliced onion
2 oz flour
1 tablespoon tomato purée
¼ pint plain yoghurt

Serves 6—8

1. Gently cook the chicken in sufficient water to cover, adding the bay leaf, bouquet garni and a sliced onion.
2. When tender cut the meat into pieces and place in a large casserole.
3. Make the sauce by melting the butter, blending in the flour and stirring in the chicken stock and tomato purée.
4. Bring to the boil, stirring until thickened.
5. Cool and stir in the egg yolks and yoghurt or soured cream, season and pour over the chicken.
6. Sprinkle on top soft breadcrumbs tossed in melted butter and a few blanched almonds. Lightly brown in a hot oven at 425°F., Gas No. 7. Serve with hot rice mixed with ½ lb cooked mushrooms and a tossed green salad.

This is also an excellent way to use up turkey at Christmas by pouring the sauce over the thinly cut white meat.

Mrs Diana Duff

ROLY—POLY CHICKEN IN SWEET AND SOUR SAUCE

3½—4 lb chicken
1 green pepper
4 oz cashew nuts
    salt and pepper
6 tablespoons oil
4 tablespoons tomato sauce

4 tablespoons soy sauce
4 oz mushrooms
¼ level teaspoon mixed spice
2 eggs
2 tomatoes
1 level tablespoon sugar

Serves 6

1. Allow chicken to thaw out completely if frozen, cut into 6 joints and remove skin and bones.
2. Marinate the meat in soy sauce for 15 minutes.
3. Wash and finely chop the green pepper, removing the core and seeds; rinse and finely chop the mushrooms. Finely chop the nuts.
4. Put the green pepper, mushrooms and nuts in a bowl, add mixed spice, salt and pepper, beat the eggs and add to the ingredients to bind the mixture together.
5. Take the chicken pieces, keeping the marinade for the sauce, and place some of the stuffing on each. Roll pieces up and secure with a cocktail stick on either end.
6. Place the chicken pieces on a greased baking tray. Brush with oil. Bake for 1 hour at 325°F., Gas No. 3.
7. Meanwhile, skin and chop the tomatoes and place in a pan with the soy sauce, tomato sauce, sugar and ½ pint of water.
8. Heat, stirring all the time, until the sauce thickens slightly. When the chicken is cooked, pour the sauce into a jug and serve it with the chicken.

Christopher Appleyard

LEMON CHICKEN

2½–3 lb chicken in portions
1 teaspoon salt
2 teaspoons paprika

2 oz plain flour
¼ teaspoon pepper

Sauce

½ cup butter
½ teaspoon pepper
¼ cup salad oil

½ teaspoon salt
2 fluid oz or
½ cup lemon juice
2 teaspoons grated lemon rind

Serves 6

1. Mix flour, salt, pepper and paprika and coat the chicken pieces.
2. Lay the pieces, skin side down, in a greased ovenproof dish large enough to take them in a single layer.
3. For the sauce, melt the butter and combine it with the salt, pepper, oil, lemon juice and lemon rind.
4. Spoon over the chicken and bake uncovered at 400°F., Gas No. 6 for 30 minutes.
5. Turn the pieces over, baste with the sauce and cook for a further 20 minutes, basting again occasionally.

This dish can be served hot or cold.

FRICASSEE OF VEAL

3 lb chopped lean veal
  without the bone
  a pinch thyme, marjoram,
  parsley
½ pint white wine
2 oz butter
  juice of 1 orange

3 medium onions, sliced
1 pint stock
20 whole peppercorns
4 cloves
3 egg yolks
4 tablespoons cream
  parsley to garnish

Serves 6

1. Put the veal, onions, herbs, peppercorns, cloves and stock into a saucepan, bring to the boil and simmer for 2 hours or until tender.

2. Season to taste, strain, but reserve stock, and keep hot.
3. In a double boiler put the butter, veal stock, wine and more herbs and bring to the boil, letting it reduce rapidly for about 10 minutes.
4. Meanwhile beat up the egg yolks with cream and add them gradually to the sauce seeing that it thickens but does not curdle. Stir it well all the time.
5. Then add the veal, stirring well. Just before serving add a good squeeze of orange juice.

This recipe is adapted from *The Closet Opened* by Sir Kenelm Digby, who lived near Sherborne from 1603 to 1665. He was a remarkable scientist and was the first person to explain the necessity of oxygen to the existence of plants. *The Closet Opened* published after his death, is full of cures, physics and recipes.

HONEYED LAMB

4—5 lb leg or shoulder of lamb
sprig of fresh rosemary or
1 teaspoon dried rosemary
1 teaspoon ground ginger

3—4 tablespoons honey (runny)
salt and freshly ground black
pepper
½ pint cider

Serves 6—8

1. Place the lamb in an ovenproof dish and sprinkle with salt, pepper and ginger.
2. Pour the honey over the lamb and lay a sprig of rosemary on top of the joint.
3. Pour the cider round the joint.
4. Cover and roast for 30 minutes at 425°F., Gas No. 7.
5. Reduce to 400°F., Gas No. 6 and allow 20 minutes to the pound plus 20 minutes extra. Baste regularly during cooking and add extra cider if necessary.
6. Uncover the joint 30 minutes before the end of cooking time.
7. Serve the juices as gravy, lightly thickened if preferred.

Mrs J. Austin

43

MONSIEUR CLAYEUX'S ROAST LAMB

1½ lb lamb, half shoulder or half a small leg (the unbony end)
3 cloves garlic
2 lb potatoes
¾ pint water
2 bay leaves
1 tablespoon salt
3 medium onions
½ teaspoon black pepper
2 oz margarine

Serves 4

1. Slice the potatoes and onions and lay them in the meat-roasting tin.
2. Sprinkle on a level tablespoon of salt and the chopped garlic (only 1½ cloves) and mix all together with the hands.
3. Rub the joint with more salt and pepper.
4. Make 3 slits in the meat and tuck a piece of garlic into each.
5. Lay the meat on the vegetables and tuck a bay leaf under each end. Dot the joint with margarine and pour the water over.
6. Put the pan on a high heat on top of the stove and bring the mixture to the boil. Put it in the oven (475°F., Gas No. 9) and baste frequently for 40 minutes.
7. Then carve the meat removing the pieces of garlic and serve the meat on a bed of the marvellous potato and onion mixture.

A French chef devised this scrumptious way of making a week's war-time meat ration for 4 people go a long way.

Mrs Pamela Duff

LAMB CHOPS IN PIQUANT SAUCE

2 lamb chops
1 oz butter
3 tablespoons redcurrant jelly

1 tablespoon Worcester sauce
juice of half a lemon
pinch of nutmeg

1. Place lamb chops in a casserole dish with 1 oz butter.
2. Mix together redcurrant jelly, Worcester sauce, lemon and nutmeg.
3. Pour the sauce over the lamb chops and cook for 1½ hours at 325°F., Gas No. 3.

Mrs B. N. Bradfield

DORSET BRAISED BEEF WITH PRUNES STUFFED WITH WALNUTS

3 lb stewing beef cut into cubes
1 tablespoon dripping or 2 tablespoons oil

1 heaped tablespoon flour
4 cloves
1 large sliced onion

1 clove garlic crushed
½ pint dark beer or stout
1 cup soaked, partly cooked and stoned prunes, or tin of prunes
12 walnuts (approximately)
salt and pepper

Serves 6

1. Heat the fat and fry the beef pieces in it, then add onion and let it soften.
2. Shake the flour over and mix well; then add the clove of garlic, cloves, salt, pepper and beer.
3. Let it bubble up, and if the sauce seems too thick add about ½ cup of water or stock.
4. Put in a casserole dish and braise in a slow oven (325°F., Gas No. 3) for 2½ hours.
5. ½ hour before it's ready, place the walnuts in the prunes and add them to the beef. Leave the lid off and continue cooking.

Also excellent for pork chops, and if a rabbit is cooked in this way it tastes very like pheasant.

HOMEMADE VIENNA STEAKS

½ lb lean minced beef
½ oz dripping
1 small egg
1 oz chopped onion

4 oz breadcrumbs
2 tablespoons cold water
salt and pepper

Serves 4

1. Cook the onions in the dripping without colouring.
2. Add to the rest of the ingredients and mix in well.
3. Divide into 4 even pieces and using a little flour, make into balls, flatten and shape into rounds.
4. Shallow fry in hot fat on both sides, reducing the heat after the first few minutes, making certain that they cook right through.

Serve with Piquant Sauce.

PIQUANT SAUCE

2 oz chopped shallots or
  onions
2 tablespoons vinegar

½ pint gravy or stock
1 oz chopped gherkins
½ teaspoon each of chopped
  chervil, tarragon and parsley

1. Place the vinegar and shallots in a small saucepan and reduce by half.
2. Add the gravy and simmer for 10 to 15 minutes.
3. Add the rest of the ingredients.
4. Skim and correct the seasoning.

Mr R. T. Chamberlain

RICH ROAST BRISKET

2—3 lb boned and rolled piece of brisket (not too fat)
1 teaspoon cornflour
1 beef stock cube or ¾ pint good stock

Serves 6

1. Place the meat in a roasting tin, uncovered and fat side up (add no fat and at this stage no liquid).
2. Cook in a preheated oven at 450°F., Gas No. 8 for 30 minutes, then lower heat to 300°F., Gas No. 2 and continue cooking for 2½—3 hours.
3. 15 minutes before the end of the cooking time mix the cornflour with cold water to a cream and pour on the boiling stock.
4. Without removing any of the fat which has come from the joint, pour the cornflour and stock round the joint (not over) and allow this liquid to boil for at least 10 minutes.
5. Dish up the joint and keep warm. Scrape the dish well, and serve the liquid as gravy, which needs no additives.

The most valuable gift that a friend can give is a good recipe. I have never ceased to be grateful to the friend who gave me this one! Follow it exactly and you will dish up roast beef as tasty and tender as any sirloin and at less than half the price. It is delicious hot and excellent cold.

Mrs Olive Howell

DORSET JUGGED STEAK

1½ lb beef steak	*1 oz flour*
1 onion	*6 cloves*
1 wine glass of port	*salt and pepper*
redcurrant jelly	*pinch of herbs*
forcemeat balls	

Serves 4

1. Cut the beef steak into pieces, dust with flour and put in a casserole.
2. Stick cloves in the onion and add with the wine, herbs and seasoning to the casserole.
3. Cook gently until the meat is tender.

Serve from the casserole with small forcemeat balls and redcurrant jelly. A similar quantity of water or stock may be substituted for the wine.

MEAT LOAF IN PASTRY

Pastry
10 oz plain flour
1 teaspoon salt
6 oz butter cut in small
  pieces
1 egg
5 oz carton soured cream
  a little beaten egg

Filling
2 lb finely minced beef
¼ mushrooms, finely chopped
2 onions, finely chopped
  salt, pepper
  few drops Worcester sauce
4 tablespoons chopped parsley
  small tin tomato purée
2 beaten eggs

1. Sift the flour and salt into a bowl, add the butter and then rub in quickly until the mixture resembles fine breadcrumbs.
2. Mix the egg and soured cream, stir into the flour mixture and work into a soft pliable ball.
3. Knead lightly, wrap in foil, and let it rest in fridge for about 1 hour.
4. Put meat into pan with chopped mushrooms and onions, stir over heat until it starts to brown, then cook until it is well browned all over, adding up to 2 tablespoons of water to prevent it going dry.
5. Scrape it into a bowl and stir in seasoning, parsley, tomato purée and beaten eggs. Make sure that it is well seasoned and then leave it to get cold.
6. Cut pastry in half and roll it into 2 rectangles about 6 x 14 inches. Lay one piece on lightly greased baking sheet and put meat mixture in centre.
7. Shape it into a long narrow loaf leaving a margin of pastry all round. Dampen edge and put second layer on top. Seal edges well, make a few slashes in the top and decorate with pastry leaves.
8. Brush with beaten egg all over and bake at 375°F., Gas No. 5 for about an hour until browned.

This is nice either hot with gravy or cold sliced for a picnic. It is a very tasty but economical recipe for a large family, especially when *all* their friends are there at once as it provides about 24 portions.

Mrs Diana Duff

1 thick slice topside, without
   fat, 3—4 inches thick weigh-
   ing about 3 lb
1 bottle good wine vinegar
   a chunk of green bacon, uncooked 4 inch sq
2—4 heads garlic
2 large onions
2 large carrots
   a handful flour
   a wine glass olive oil
   a pinch nutmeg
3 to 4 cloves
2 teaspoons sugar
1 tumbler Madeira or sweet sherry
3 tumblers good homemade sugo
12 soaked, stoned prunes

Sugo
2 lb fresh tomatoes or
1 large tin
½ lb onions
½ lb celery
½ lb carrots
2 teaspoons sugar
1 tablespoon olive oil
1 pint strong stock
   herbs to taste

Serves 6

1. Marinade the beef in a bowl for 24 hours using enough
   wine vinegar to cover it. Turn the meat over once or twice
   during this process.
   Remove it and pat dry with a clean cloth.
2. Cut up the garlic into thin slivers the length of the clove.
3. Cut up the bacon into larding strips about 2 inches long and
   the thickness of a pencil.
4. Make a deep slit in the side of the meat with a suitable
   narrow, sharp and pointed knife. Insert a piece of bacon
   and a sliver of garlic into this slit pushing them both well
   into the centre of the meat. Continue larding all the way
   round the sides and then see if you can fit in another row,
   maybe above or below the first one, but do not pierce the
   top or bottom surface of the meat.
5. When all the bacon and garlic is used up and the meat is fit
   to burst put a large handful of flour on a plate, and flour
   both sides of the meat well.

Continued

6. Chop the onions and carrots roughly and put them into a heavy iron and enamel casserole pan with a wine glass of good olive oil. Add 3 cloves, a good pinch of nutmeg and 2 teaspoons sugar.
7. When the onion has softened but not darkened, add the meat, and sauté it well, turning it over carefully several times until it is well coloured on every side. This will take at least 10 minutes
8. Add a tumbler of Madeira and let it cook a little longer, turning it over once more.
9. Pour in at least 3 tumblers of good tomato sugo (previously prepared from above ingredients, all simmered together for several hours) enough to cover the meat well.
10. Cook for a few minutes, then add the prunes, stir and cover the pan. Continue simmering for roughly 2 hours or until the meat is tender. You can top up the sauce with more sugo or a little stock if necessary.
11. Take the meat out and put it on a flat hot serving dish. Slice it vertically about the thickness of a little finger, so each piece of larding shows. Pour half the sauce over the meat. Pour the other half into a sauce-boat (scraping the pan for all juices). Serve with buttered noodles or fettucini.

This dish comes from the island of Korcula in Yugoslavia.

Derek Nimmo

BOBOTIE
Prounced BO (as in Bob), BOT (as in lure) TIE (as in tea)

2 *lb minced meat*	1 *thick slice of bread*
2 *teaspoons curry powder*	1 *dessertspoon sugar*
2 *tablespoons dripping*	½ *cup vinegar*
2 *medium onions*	2 *eggs*
1 *cup hot milk*	*salt and pepper*
1 *dessertspoon apricot jam*	
1 *grated apple*	

Serves 6—8

1. Brown the chopped onion in hot dripping, add the curry powder and the sugar.
2. Remove from the heat, add the jam, grated apple and vinegar.
3. Mix the mince with the bread soaked in hot milk.
4. Add salt, then curry mixture and mix well.
5. Cook in a slow oven (300°F., Gas No. 2) for about 1 hour.
6. Top with 2 eggs beaten with ½ cup milk and salt and pepper.
7. Bake in a moderate oven (350°F., Gas No. 4) until brown. Serve with boiled rice.

This delicate dish is of Malay origin and is now a traditional South African recipe. It was often cooked by travellers in an ant heap oven, i.e. an oven made out of a discarded ant heap. Today it tastes just as good baked in a modern oven. The ant heaps are made and then vacated by the ants — they can be quite high and are as hard as cement.

Mrs Sandra Ellis

JAMBON MICHODIERE (NORMANDY)

4 thick slices of ham
1 onion, finely chopped
3½ tablespoons unsalted butter
8 oz sausage meat
3½ oz seedless sultanas
3½ oz stoned and chopped
  prunes

2 bananas, thinly sliced
2 dessert apples, thinly sliced
7 oz rough puff pastry
1 egg, beaten
2 tablespoons Calvados or a
  little cider
tomato sauce

Serves 4

1. Gently fry the onion in the melted butter. Add the sausage meat and the fruit.
2. Mix with a wooden spoon, cover and leave to simmer gently for 20 minutes, stirring frequently.
3. Butter a flan dish, spread half the mixture over it.
4. Arrange the ham slices on top, then spread the remaining mixture over the ham.
5. Cover with pastry, folding the edges back slightly towards the inside of the dish.
6. Criss-cross the pastry, brush with egg, and make a small hole in the centre. Bake in a hot oven (425°F., Gas No. 7) for about 25 minutes. Lower the temperature after 15 minutes. During the cooking pour in the Calvados. Serve with tomato sauce.

I have sometimes lined the flan dish with pastry and used this recipe cold for a picnic.

Mrs Eva Betton

PARTY PORK

4 lb chined loin of pork

Stuffing

4 oz breadcrumbs
2 level tablespoons of
   chopped gherkins
1 medium orange

1 level teaspoon of mixed
   spice
1 level tablespoon demerara
   sugar

Serves 8

1. Remove the skin and bones from the meat. Cut down into the fat through the centre of the loin, and ease the fat away from the meat about 1 inch each side of the centre cut.
2. Score the fat into diamond shapes with a sharp knife.
3. Mix all the ingredients together for stuffing, only using the rind of the orange, place into the cavity made by cutting back the fat.
4. Place in a roasting tin, pressing demerara sugar into the scored fat, squeeze orange juice over the joint and cook for 1½ hours at 375°F., Gas No. 5. Baste with remaining juice, cover stuffing with strip of foil to avoid burning and cook for a further hour.

PORK CHOPS WITH BARBECUE SAUCE

4 loin pork chops

Topping

2 oz white bread
1 teaspoon grated lemon
   rind

1 teaspoon parsley
1 small onion, sliced
   salt and pepper

Sauce

1 small onion, sliced
1 oz butter
3 level tablespoons soft
   brown sugar
3 tablespoons tomato
   ketchup

1 small green pepper
2 tablespoons malt vinegar
½ teaspoon dry mustard
1 tablespoon Worcester
   sauce
¼ pint water

Continued

1. Prepare the chops.
2. Crumble topping ingredients together in the liquidiser.
3. Chop the onion and pepper and fry in butter for 5 minutes.
4. Put into liquidiser with remaining sauce ingredients and blend till smooth.
5. Brown the chops in hot fat—drain and place in a shallow oven-proof dish. Pour the sauce over and spread each chop with the crumb mixture.
6. Cover and cook in a 375°F., Gas No. 5 oven for 30 minutes, uncover and cook for another 20 minutes.

This dish is equally good with chicken joints.

Mrs F. Buchanan

PORK FILLETS WITH CIDER

2—3 pork fillets according to size
1 small onion
¼ pint dry cider
kneaded butter
a few outside leaves of celery

1—2 tablespoons oil
½ oz butter
1 tart cooking apple
¼ pint stock
1 dessertspoon chopped parsley

Serves 6

1. Brown the fillets all over in the oil and butter.
2. Take out, and fry the onion, finely chopped and the apple quartered, cored and sliced. Fry for a few minutes.
3. Replace the fillets, add the cider and a little stock.
4. Season, cover and simmer for 25 minutes or until tender.
5. Take up the fillets and slice diagonally.
6. Keep warm, strain the gravy, return to the pan and thicken with a little kneaded butter. Adjust seasoning, add parsley and replace the pork. Heat gently and serve.

The dish may be garnished with rings of fried apple and with a lentil purée into which a little chopped raw celery has been stirred just before serving.

Mrs P. Ward

PORK CHOPS WITH ORANGE AND GINGER

2 lean pork chops
2 oz soft brown sugar
¼ level teaspoon ground
  ginger
1 small orange

½ oz butter
3 tablespoons wine vinegar
salt
freshly milled pepper
2 level teaspoons cornflour

1. Trim the chops and add to the hot melted butter in a frying pan. Fry over medium heat until the chops are well browned on both sides. Then pour away excess fat from the pan.
2. Blend the brown sugar, vinegar, ginger and a little salt and pepper in a basin.
3. Cut 4 slices from the orange.
4. Pour the vinegar and sugar mixture over the chops in the pan.
5. Top each chop with 2 of the orange slices.
6. Squeeze any juice from the remaining orange into the pan. Cover with a lid and leave to simmer gently for about 30 minutes.
7. Lift the chops on to a hot serving dish.
8. Drain off the pan liquid, measure and make up to ¼ pint with water. Blend the cornflour with a little cold water until smooth and then stir into the pan liquid. Return the mixture to the frying pan and stir over the heat until the sauce is boiling and has thickened. Strain over the chops and serve.

Mrs P. Ward

PORK WITH PLUMS

1 lb plums
1 lemon
  pinch of powdered
  ginger

1 teaspoon caster sugar
½ cup demerara sugar
6 spare-rib chops of pork
1 onion

Serves 6

1. Stone the plums and cook with caster sugar, juice of lemon, brown sugar and pinch of ginger for 10 minutes or until the plums are soft.
2. Remove the plums and add the onion, finely chopped, to the juice and cook slowly for 5—10 minutes.
3. Coat the chops with this mixture, seal the casserole well and cook for 1—1½ hours in a hot oven (400°F., Gas No. 6) until the chops are tender.

This recipe gives a very interesting and tasty effect to the chops.

Mrs M. Willmott

JENI'S DUCKLING

2 5—6 lb ducklings
2 tablespoons vinegar
2 celery sticks, finely
  chopped
  juice and grated rind
  of 2 oranges
1 oz butter
  salt and pepper
1 bay leaf
1 orange

2 tablespoons granulated
  sugar
1 medium onion, finely
  chopped
½ pint stock
1 tablespoon brandy
3 oz flaked almonds
1 sprig of parsley
  watercress

Serves 8

1. Preheat oven to 400°F., Gas No. 6. Prick the birds and put in the oven for 1 hour in total, for first ½ hour with legs upwards, and right side up for last ½ hour.
2. Remove the ducks from the oven, drain and joint. Put in a clean roasting pan, skin side up.

3. Put sugar and vinegar into a thick pan, and boil until caramelised. Pour on the stock (cover your hands as it will spit), stir until the lumps disappear. Add the orange rind and juice, and brandy and pour over the duck; cook in the oven for about 20 minutes. Do *not* baste. Remove the joints and keep warm in the oven (if the skin is not crisp, pop in the oven for 10 more minutes).
4. Fry flaked almonds in butter until brown.
5. Scatter over the duck.
6. Skim the sauce. Strain into pan. Add finely chopped celery and onion. Boil for about 5 minutes. Season and serve with orange slices and watercress as decoration.

Really tasty and different.

Mrs Jeni Atherton

PIGEON D'ABBE

Serves 8

1. Collect, by some means, 8 pigeons, preferably from the precincts of the Abbey.
2. Pluck them. Some people peel them, using only the breasts, but I think this is no quicker. Taking the wings off with a pair of secateurs, the bird can be plucked in about 3 minutes. So pluck and clean and apart from the above dish, there is material for soup at a later date.
3. Pressure cook the pigeons in well flavoured stock with a glass of red cooking wine for about 40 minutes.
4. Remove the pigeons and carefully remove their breasts.
5. Make a thickish sauce with the butter and the flour and the stock. When the flavour and the consistency are right, add chopped mushrooms. Do not cook too long, just long enough for the sauce to take on a light grey colour. Let it rest for a few minutes then add the cream, reheat but do not boil. Then sit down and enjoy it.

Paul Goddard
Vicar of Sherborne

CASEROLE OF PHEASANT

1 pheasant	1 onion
2 tablespoons brandy	2 tablespoons olive oil
1 small carton cream	salt, pepper, fresh thyme

Serves 4

1. Put the pheasant in a heavy casserole with a whole onion.
2. Cover with 2 tablespoons olive oil, salt, pepper and fresh thyme. Put the casserole in the oven for about 1½ hours at 350°F., Gas No. 4.
3. Then add 2 tablespoons of brandy. Cook a little longer (this dish will wait till you are ready for it) and just before serving add 1 small carton of cream.

A good disguise for a tough old bird!

Mrs Polly Anderson

TOURTIERES – FRENCH CANADIAN

½ lb minced beef	½ lb minced pork
1 medium onion, finely chopped	½ teaspoon salt
	¼ teaspoon pepper
¼ teaspoon celery salt	¼ teaspoon cloves
¼ pint water	pastry for a 9 inch 2–crust pie

Serves 4–6

1. Mix the beef and pork and dry ingredients, then add water.
2. Cook in a saucepan until the surplus water is reduced, but not dry. Cool.
3. Divide the pastry into two, roll out, line a shallow pie dish.
4. Put in the filling and cover with pastry.
5. Cook at 450°F., Gas No. 8 for 10 minutes. Reduce heat to 350°F., Gas No. 4 and cook for 40 minutes or until the pastry is done.

Miss G. Murphy

SEVEN LAYER DINNER

a layer of thinly sliced raw potatoes
a layer of thinly sliced raw onion
a layer of thinly sliced raw carrot
a small cup of uncooked rice
a tin of peas, together with the liquid
a tin of tomato soup, and add a tin full of water
a layer of sausages (these should be cut into thirds and stuck in upright all over the surface)

1. Place the ingredients layer by layer in a casserole in the above order.
2. Put into a medium oven (375°F., Gas No. 5) with lid on for one hour, and then remove the lid and continue cooking for a further hour at 350°F., Gas No. 4.

This can be made in any size of casserole according to need, so no quantities are specified. If a small casserole is used obviously small tins of soup and peas are required, and a smaller quantity of rice, and cooking time slightly reduced.

Lady Fisher

SAVOURY LIVER

½ lb lamb liver   *1 medium onion*
2 tablespoons tomato purée   *1 stock cube*
¼ lb mushrooms   *1 small carton soured cream*

Serves 2

1. Chop the onion and cook until soft in a little oil.
2. Add the chopped mushrooms, tomato purée and crumbled stock cube, stirring frequently to prevent sticking.
3. Cut the liver into matchstick-sized pieces, add to the other ingredients and cook until they are soft.
4. Remove from the heat and add soured cream slowly, stirring all the time to prevent curdling.

Mrs Jean Roberts

FARMHOUSE CASSEROLE

2 rabbits
½ cup milk

½ lb bacon

Stuffing
½ lb breadcrumbs
2 tablespoons chopped
parsley
good pinch of pepper
1 egg

1 tablespoon chopped onion
1 tablespoon mixed herbs
1 tablespoon chopped candied
peel

Serves 6

To make the stuffing

Mix all the ingredients with the well-beaten egg. Do not add butter or dripping.

To make the casserole

1. Skin and wash rabbits, cut into joints and place in a casserole.
2. Sprinkle over and round them the stuffing, made as above. Lay on top of the stuffing the bacon, cut into pieces.
3. Pour the milk over all, put on the lid and bake in the oven for 2½ hours at 350°F., Gas No. 4.

The Yetties

DORSET FAGGOTS

½ lb pig or lamb liver
1 lb lean belly of pork
2 oz suet
sage
4 largish onions, peeled
and sliced
½ teaspoon salt
1 Oxo cube mixed in a jug
with ½—1 pint boiling
water

1 lb pork sausage meat
some ketcher (caul fat)
½ lb breadcrumbs
4 large cooking apples, peeled
and cored
½ teaspoon allspice
¼ teaspoon pepper

Makes 12—14

1. Mince the liver, sausage meat, belly pork and suet.
2. Grind the bread and the sage in a liquidiser and add to the minced meat in a large bowl.
3. Add the allspice, salt and pepper and mix well.
4. Put the ketcher in a basin of warm water, and with scissors cut into small pieces to hold the mince, and lay around the basin edge.
5. Put the pieces in the palm of the hand and a good tablespoon of mince, making the size you want.
6. Place them in a baking dish and cover ¾ of the faggots with the Oxo gravy.
7. Cook in a hot oven (400°F., Gas No. 6) for at least an hour or until nicely brown. They are better well cooked. Serve with peas and apple sauce.

Mrs K. Millard

SHERBORNE ABBEY

Sherborne Abbey,
So gold and bright,
God will be sad if you die,
Your roof so tumbled about
Poor old Abbey —
Hope you live.

Nicole Peall   *age 8*

Light Lunches and Suppers

FRENCH RECIPE FOR COLD SALMON AND RICE MAYONNAISE

salmon   *rice*
mayonnaise   *relish*
salt

1. Take equal quantities of cold, flaked salmon and cold, cooked rice.
2. Mix the rice with the salmon and bind with mayonnaise.
3. Season to taste with either mustard, cayenne pepper, Worcester sauce or *sauce diable.*
4. Put the mixture in a mould or basin and keep in the bottom of the fridge until required. Garnish with sliced tomatoes, sprigs of parsley and sliced cucumber. Add more mayonnaise just before serving.

Mrs Meg Whittingdale

SMOKED HADDOCK MOUSSE

12 oz smoked haddock fillet (cooked and flaked)
½ pint mayonnaise
¼ pint light stock
½ pint double cream lightly whipped

2 hard-boiled eggs (chopped)
¼ pint cold Bechamel sauce
½ oz gelatine soaked in ½ cup of cold water

Serves 4

1. Mix the sauce and mayonnaise together.
2. Dissolve the gelatine in the water over low heat and set on one side.
3. Add the flaked fish and chopped egg to the sauce mixture followed by the stock, gelatine (cool) and the lightly whipped cream.
4. Turn into a dish and leave to set. Decorate with sliced lemon (and caviare!).

Mrs Buchanan

TUNA ELLERY QUEEN

1 medium tin of tuna fish
1 small onion
1 lemon
2 tablespoons mayonnaise

1 green pepper
1 head of celery
oregano, thyme, Worcester
sauce, English mustard

Serves 4

1. Turn out the tuna, add the finely chopped onion, celery and green pepper, juice of half the lemon, freshly ground pepper, salt, dash of Worcester sauce, half a teaspoon dry mustard and a pinch of oregano and thyme.
2. Bind with mayonnaise.
3. Heap in a bowl, cover with foil and chill.
4. Serve accompanied by brown bread and butter, or heap mounds of it on hot toast as individual servings.

This recipe for a main dish salad was found in a book by Ellery Queen, the American detective story writer. The salad was given to the murderer's victim, but the poison which was included in the salad, has been omitted!

Mrs Jean Curtis-Brown

CRACKERED FISH

1 lb haddock	1 oz rice per person
1 pint white sauce	¼ lb shrimps
¼ lb mushrooms	6 cream crackers, thickly
4 oz grated cheese	buttered
tomatoes for garnish	

Serves 4–6

1. Bake the haddock, reserving the juices for the sauce.
2. Cook the rice and line a dish with it.
3. Place the cream crackers sandwiched together in twos in the fridge until the butter hardens.
4. Cook the mushrooms in a little water, which should be used in the sauce.
5. Crumble the buttered biscuits with a rolling pin.
6. Make the white sauce using the fish and mushroom juices.
7. Add the shrimps and mushrooms.
8. Cover the rice with the flaked, baked haddock.
9. Pour the sauce over it.
10. Mix the crumbled biscuits and cheese and sprinkle over the fish.
11. Garnish with tomatoes and brown in the oven.

Mrs Dorothy Cottam

KATIE PIE

2 lb cooked potatoes, thinly sliced	1 small cup cooked fish
	2 hard-boiled eggs

For sauce

1 kipper, cooked, boned and chopped	1 small onion
	1 oz margarine
1 oz flour	1 cup milk
1 cup grated cheese	salt and pepper

Serves 4–6

1. Line a greased casserole or dish with the potatoes, leaving a few aside to top the dish.
2. Add the cooked fish and hard-boiled eggs, sliced.

3. Fry the onion in the margarine until soft, add the flour and milk.
4. Stir in the kipper that has been cooked, boned and chopped. Season with pepper and salt.
5. Pour half this sauce over the eggs and potatoes in the casserole, sprinkle with a little cheese.
6. Cover with a thin layer of sliced potatoes, the rest of the sauce, and top with more potatoes covering with the rest of the cheese.
7. Dot with margarine and bake until browned.

Mrs Dorothy Seddon

SEAFOOD TIMBALE

1½ lb potatoes	1 oz butter
a little milk	1 lb coley or any cheap fish
salt and pepper	½ pint milk
pinch mixed herbs	1 oz flour
1 oz dried mustard	1 oz butter
2 oz cooked ham (optional)	1 hard-boiled egg
chopped parsley	salt and pepper

Serves 4

1. Cook, drain and mash the potatoes with butter, milk and seasoning, and leave on one side.
2. Cook the fish in ¼ pint milk and 1 oz butter until tender.
3. Flake on to a plate removing bones and skin.
4. Mix the flour, mustard, salt and pepper in a bowl with the remaining milk and add to the rest of the milk, cooking to make a white sauce.
5. Add mixed herbs, parsley, ham and chopped hard-boiled egg to the white sauce, and finally add the flaked fish, mixing well.
6. Pipe the potatoes around the dish and cover the bottom, then put in the fish mixture.
7. If this is to be used as a starter it is more effective if the fish mixture is put into individual dishes and the potatoes piped on the top. Brown under the grill before serving.

Mrs Sally Price

CURRIED FISH PIE

2 pieces smoked haddock
milk
2 hard-boiled eggs
1 tablespoon curry powder

8 oz rough puff pastry
seasoning
¾ pint white sauce

Serves 4

1. Poach the fish in milk and seasoning for approximately 15 minutes. Place fish in a pie dish.
2. Slice the eggs and put over the fish.
3. Make the white sauce and add about 1 tablespoon of curry powder.
4. Pour over the filling in the pie dish.
5. Cover the dish with the pastry and cook at 425°F., Gas No. 7 until the pastry is brown.

Husband likes it—can't be too bad.

Mrs Alison Underwood

SAUSAGE MEAT AND APPLE FLAN

1 small onion, finely
chopped
¼ teaspoon thyme
1 partially cooked short-
crust flan case

¾ lb sausage meat
1 small tin tomatoes
3 dessert apples, 2 chopped
and 1 sliced

Serves 4—6

1. Lightly fry the onion till transparent, add the sausage meat, tomatoes, thyme and chopped apple.
2. Season to taste if necessary.
3. Mix the ingredients thoroughly together and heat through.
4. Place the mixture in the flan case, decorate with apple slices and cook in moderate oven (350°F., Gas No. 4) for about 20—25 minutes.

Mrs Eve Nicoll

DORSET FLAN

Pastry
8 oz flour
4 oz butter or margarine
4 tablespoons water
   pinch of salt

Filling
4 oz cooked sliced ham
3 eggs
½ pint milk
2 teaspoons fine semolina
   salt and pepper

Serves 6

1. Make pastry and line an 8 inch flan tin.
2. Take 1 egg and beat it well, and then brush the bottom of the pastry with the beaten egg to prevent the bottom getting soggy.
3. Lay the ham slices on the pastry and then break 2 whole (unbeaten) eggs on top.
4. Mix together in a basin the semolina, milk, remainder of the beaten egg, and seasoning to taste, until it is a smooth paste.
5. Pour over the ham and eggs.
6. Bake in a moderate oven (375°F., Gas No. 5) for 30–40 minutes until the top is brown.

This flan can be eaten hot or cold, traditionally it would be served with local watercress and followed with Dorset knobs and Blue Vinny cheese.

LUXURY FRENCH ONION FLAN

Pastry
½ lb plain flour
1 rounded tablespoon icing
  sugar
5 oz butter
¼ teaspoon salt

Filling
5½ oz margarine
2 large onions
3 eggs
½ pint milk (or milk and
  cream)
1 level tablespoon flour
  salt and pepper

Serves 6—8

1. Rub the butter into the sieved flour, sugar and salt. Keep in
   fridge for at least ½ hour.
2. Press out pastry into a large 10—11 inch flan case.
3. Prick base and bake blind without beans for 10 minutes at
   475°F., Gas No. 9. Cool.
4. Chop the onions and cook gently in the margarine until transparent.
5. Stir in the flour. Beat the eggs and stir into the onions.
6. Add salt, pepper and the milk. Pour into the pastry case and
   dredge with nutmeg. Cook at 375°F., Gas No. 5 for 25—30
   minutes until set.

Mrs J. Austin

CHEESE AND CHUTNEY PIE

8 oz flaky pastry
1 oz flour
2 eggs, separated
    salt and pepper
    beaten egg to glaze

1 oz butter
½ pint milk
8 oz grated cheese
3 large tablespoons chutney
    or sweet pickle

Serves 4—6

1. Roll out half the pastry and use to line an 8 inch flan tin.
2. Make a sauce from the butter, flour and milk; when it has thickened, stir in the egg yolks and cheese and season with salt and pepper.
3. Whisk the egg whites and fold into the sauce.
4. Spread the chutney over the base of the pastry and cover with the sauce.
5. Roll out the remainder of the pastry, cover the pie, seal and decorate the edges and brush the top with beaten egg.
6. Bake near the top of the oven (425°F., Gas No. 7) for 30 minutes until golden. Serve hot or cold.

Mrs J. Davis

SURPRISE 'SAUSAGES'

1. Mix in roughly equal quantities: grated cheese, raw porridge oats, breadcrumbs (preferably brown).
2. Add enough beaten egg to make a dough.
3. Colour pink with about 2 good shakes of tomato ketchup.
4. Season as desired.
5. Shape into sausage lengths.

These may be eaten raw if wished, or fried, grilled or baked until crisp on the outside and brown. This is a very filling dish and together with a drink of orange juice it makes a complete balanced meal for a pensioner or slimmer. To add bulk to fill a family, serve with jacket potatoes or crisps and baked beans or peas.

Miss E. F. Dainty

BACON BOLSTERS

2 medium onions	1 lb mashed potatoes
4 rashers collar bacon	½ pint milk
1 oz flour	6 oz grated cheese
pinch of herbs	1 oz butter

Serves 4

1. Fry the onions in a little dripping, add the cooked mashed potatoes and the pinch of herbs and mix well.
2. Form into 4 sausage shapes and roll a rasher of bacon round each one.
3. Place in a greased ovenproof dish and cook until the bacon looks done.
4. Meanwhile make a cheese sauce with 2 oz of the cheese, milk, flour and butter.
5. When the bacon is cooked, pour the sauce over the 'sausages', sprinkle the remaining 4 oz cheese on top and cook in a moderate oven (350°F., Gas No. 4) until golden. Serve hot.

Mrs E. Rickard

BAKED POTATO WITH A DIFFERENCE

1 large potato	1 rasher streaky bacon
1 lamb kidney	small amount of made mustard

1. Bake the potato to within ½ hour of full cooking time then remove from oven.
2. Cut a cross in the skin on top, pull back the skin and press the inside down to make a well.
3. Spread mustard on the bacon, place the kidney in the middle of the rasher, roll up and secure with a cocktail stick, and put it inside the potato.
4. Press down and cover with the skin as much as possible, return to the oven and cook for another ½ hour.

Mrs Jean Roberts

CHEESE AND ONION FRITTERS

4 oz plain flour
¼ pint milk
3 oz grated Cheddar
  cheese
  fat or oil for frying

1 egg
salt and cayenne or black
pepper to taste
1 medium or small onion,
  diced or grated

Serves 3—4

1. Place the flour and seasoning in a basin, mix in the lightly beaten egg and the milk. Stir until smooth.
2. Add the cheese and onion and stir until evenly blended. The mixture should drop easily from the spoon, add a little milk if necessary.
3. Drop teaspoonsful of the mixture into the hot fat and fry until golden brown on both sides. Drain on absorbent paper and serve at once.

Mrs Susan Higginson

HAM AND CELERY HEART ROLLS

8 slices cooked ham
2 oz butter
½ (generous) pint milk
  salt and pepper

1 tin celery hearts
1 oz flour
1 glass white wine
4 oz grated cheese

Serves 4—6

1. Cut the celery hearts in half lengthwise, and roll them carefully in the ham slices.
2. Lightly butter a long shallow fireproof dish, and lay the ham rolls across.
3. Make a sauce with the butter, flour, milk, wine, seasoning and most of the cheese, and cover the ham rolls with the sauce.
4. Sprinkle the cheese on top and bake in a moderate oven (350°F., Gas No. 4) for about 20 minutes, until lightly browned.

Mrs Julia Wallen

6 *large aubergines*   2 *large Spanish onions*
2 *cloves garlic*   6 *large ripe tomatoes*
2 *tablespoons fresh parsley* ½ *pint oil*
   salt, pepper and a little
   sugar

Serves 6

1. Cut the aubergines in half lengthways. Scoop out some of the flesh leaving a firm hollow shell.
2. Sprinkle them with salt and set aside for about 20 minutes.
3. Chop the onions and sauté them in a tablespoon of oil until they are soft, but not browned.
4. Add the skinned, deseeded and chopped tomatoes, also the garlic (pressed or finely chopped), the parsley and the aubergine flesh, and sauté all together for a few moments.
5. Wash the salt out of the aubergine shells and dry them. Spoon in the tomatoes etc., and sprinkle with a little salt, pepper and sugar.
6. Pour the rest of the oil into a deep ovenproof dish, which will hold the aubergines laid neatly and carefully side by side. Bake for 1½ hours at 325°F., Gas No. 3 or until tender.
7. Remove the aubergines very carefully to a serving dish. Keep the oil to use again as it has a lovely flavour.

This is a Turkish dish of stuffed aubergines. It is called *Imam Baildi* which means literally the swooning Imam—the priest having fainted at the first taste of this wondrous dish.

Mrs Pamela Duff

JANSSONS FRESTELSE (Jansson's Temptation)

5—6 *medium potatoes*   1½ *oz butter*
2—3 *onions sliced*   10 *tinned anchovy fillets*
½ *pint single cream*

Serves 4

1. Peel the potatoes and cut into fine strips.
2. Soak to remove starch.
3. Fry the onion in butter until golden brown.
4. Dry potatoes.
5. Grease an ovenproof dish. Put potatoes, onions and anchovies in the dish in layers and pour half the cream over.
6. Dot with butter and cook in a moderate oven (350°F., Gas No. 4) for about 30 minutes.
7. Pour remaining cream over and bake for a further 20 minutes.

This is a Swedish supper dish, or a special way of cooking potatoes for a main meal.

Mrs I. Davies

INDIAN POTATO DISH

2 onions
½ teaspoon ground chilli
  powder
4 eggs

2 oz fat or lard
1 teaspoon turmeric powder
1 lb diced cooked potatoes
  garlic and parsley

Serves 4

1. Partly fry 2 onions in the fat.
2. Add ½ teaspoon ground chilli powder and 1 teaspoon turmeric powder.
3. Continue frying until lightly brown.
4. Add 1 lb diced cooked potatoes and mix.
5. Beat 4 eggs with pepper and a little salt and pour over potato mixture.
6. Cook until eggs are just set. Serve at once. Garlic and parsley may be added according to taste.

This is a versatile dish and other vegetables can be substituted for the potato, e.g. peas, broad beans, peppers, diced carrots, etc.

Steve Underwoood

KROPPKAKON

10—12 medium potatoes,
  boiled
½ teaspoon salt

1 egg
5 oz flour

Filling
  fried bacon and onion
  black pepper

Serves 6—8

1. Mash the potatoes and mix with the egg, flour and salt.
2. Make into a long flat sausage and slice.
3. Fill each slice with some of the filling mixture and seal by forming into dumplings.
4. Boil the dumplings in plenty of salted water. They are cooked when they float.
5. Serve with melted butter and redcurrant jelly. Alternatively, cool after boiling and then fry.

Mrs Mary Lock

CHINESE CABBAGE A LA WHEATSHEAF

½ Chinese cabbage leaves,
  shredded
  large dollop of butter
  bacon and sausages
  fried and coarsely chopped

1 large onion, sliced
3 sticks celery, sliced
  salt and freshly ground
  pepper

Serves 2

1. Sauté the onion in butter.
2. When soft and golden add chopped cabbage, celery and seasoning.
3. Turn in butter; cover and cook over a low heat for 10—15 minutes (or longer if cabbage preferred soft).
4. Add bacon and sausages and serve.

Miss June Barbour

QUICK PIZZA

For the dough
8 oz self-raising flour
   pinch of salt
1 level teaspoon dry
   mustard
1½ oz butter
2 oz finely grated cheese
¼ pint milk

For the topping
8 slices cheese
4—5 tablespoons tomato
   ketchup
8 anchovy fillets (if liked)
4 olives (stuffed or plain)
Optional additions
   oregano, fresh tomato slices,
   basil, parmesan, garlic

Serves 6

1. Mix the flour and salt and rub in the butter.
2. Stir in the cheese and mustard, and mix with enough milk to make a light pliable dough.
3. Roll out the dough to 9 inches diameter.
4. Bake in a hot oven (425°F., Gas No. 7) for 15—20 minutes.
5. Cover with the topping and put back in the oven for 5 minutes more.

TO MAKE A HARTY CHOKE PIE

Take one dozen bottomes of ye harty chokes that are not full ripe cut them and boil them to that purpose but not over tender then take a pint of whit wine, ¾ lb sugar, large mace, a good quantity on dozens of dates, season ye bottomes with nutmeg and salte a littel and a very littel pepper put all these into a puter dish and let it stand on a chafing dish of coales and stue to howers then set it by being cloz covered when you put them into ye pie take ye bottomes from ye liquer with ye mace and dates and put to them good store of marrow and fresh butter for ye liquer put not that in till ye pie be hard which will be in half an hower and after ye liquer is in let it stand so much longer than take it for your use.

This is from Mary Lyford's receipt book who was the cook for the family of William Lyford who was a minister of the gospel at Sherborne from 1631—53. However, times change and now 330 years later ministers of the gospel are more self-sufficient...

8—10 cooked globe artichoke
  hearts
¼—½ lb Gruyere cheese
1 oz butter
½—¾ pint milk

1—1½ lb of small new potatoes,
  do not scrape or peel,
  simply wash and cook
1 oz flour

Serves 6—8

1. Cook the artichokes and the potatoes. Place in a dish, preferably earthenware.
2. Make a sauce with the cheese, butter, flour and milk, and pour it over the artichokes and potatoes.
3. Then forget about it until about an hour before lunch the following day. Place it in a moderate oven (350°F., Gas No. 4) and cook for about ¾ hour. Serve with a salad.

A delicious lunch with a glass of light cider. Nuns are very useful people, especially French nuns, not only because of their prayers but because they cook well. At the Abbey in Bec Herllouin in Normandy where I spend a lot of time, the nuns serve this delicious dish for lunch sometimes. Alas I do not know what it is called but it is superb. I will call it Artichoke and Potato Pie.

Rev. John Eley

Puddings

LEMON SURPRISE PUDDING

2 oz butter
2 eggs
½ pint milk

3½ oz sugar
2 oz self-raising flour
1 lemon

Serves 4—6

1. Cream the butter with the grated rind of a lemon and the sugar.
2. When it is fluffy beat in 2 egg yolks, then stir in alternately the flour and just under ½ pint milk.
3. Add the juice of the lemon and fold in the stiffly beaten egg whites, lightly but thoroughly.
4. Bake in a moderate oven (350°F., Gas No. 4) for about 45 minutes until the pudding is golden brown.

Underneath the sponge topping there will be a creamy lemon sauce.

RUSSIAN ICE

*2 handfuls young black-
currant leaves*
*4 large lemons
whipping cream for
serving*

½ lb white sugar
1 pint water
2 egg whites

Serves 8

1. Dissolve the sugar in a pan with the water, boil and make a syrup.
2. Into this throw the blackcurrant leaves.
3. Remove the pan from the heat and infuse with the lid on for 2 hours.
4. Strain off the leaves and add the juice of the lemons to the syrup.
5. Freeze for 2—3 hours or until the mixture is firm.
6. Mash well with a fork and add the egg whites stiffly whisked.
7. Return to the fridge until ready to serve. Serve with whipped cream.

Dame Diana Reader Harris

AUNTY MARGARET'S PUDDING

4 oz flour	2 oz sugar
2 oz butter or margarine	1 egg
¼ pint milk (approximately)	

Serves 4–6

1. Rub the butter into the flour.
2. Add the sugar.
3. Lightly beat the eggs, and with the milk add to the dry ingredients and mix together until you have a smooth, thick batter consistency.
4. Put 3 tablespoons of jam in a greased basin, and pour the mixture in leaving a good inch at the top to allow the pudding to rise.
5. Steam or boil for 1½ hours.

This recipe is almost a hundred years old and on first reading, the ingredients and method appear so simple that it seems nothing special. But the result is a very light and delicious pudding, which has the added attraction of being economical. One last note in the recipe book: 'I find steaming best, and do not shake the saucepan or it will go heavy.' Be warned!

Mrs Newman

BAKED LEMON PUDDING

2 eggs, separated	3 oz sugar
2 oz plain flour	pinch of salt
½ pint milk	small lemon

Serves 4

1. Beat the egg yolks and add sugar, salt and flour. Mix well.
2. Stir in the milk, grated lemon rind and juice.
3. Fold in the stiffly beaten egg whites.
4. Pour into a greased pie dish and set in a tin in about 1 inch of water. Bake at 350°F., Gas No. 4 for about 50 minutes.

Mrs Marion Baker

MY GRANDMOTHER'S PLUM PUDDING

1½ lb raisins

½ lb mixed peel

¾ lb suet

1 wine glass brandy

½ lb currants

¾ lb breadcrumbs

8 eggs

1 lb sugar

Each pudding serves 8

This is my grandmother's recipe, and no method is given in her recipe book. I mix it all together after chopping the raisins, put it into two 7 inch basins and steam or boil for 6—8 hours.

This recipe has been used every year in our family since about 1860 and is delicious. The modern plum pudding was taken from the old plum-porridge which was made of boiled beef or mutton, with broth thickened with brown bread to which was added, when boiled, raisins, prunes, ginger, mace, currants and cloves.

Mrs J. M. Loxton

BOUBELARDS (My special)

1 egg, well beaten

½ teacup milk

flour

½ lb lard for frying

caster sugar for coating

a little nutmeg

Serves 4

1. Add enough flour, gradually, to the egg, milk and nutmeg, and make a thin batter as for pancakes. This mixture is improved by standing for ½ hour.
2. Put the lard into a saucepan and bring to the boil. Drop a dessertspoon of the batter into the boiling lard. It will rise quickly and keep turning round, then over, so that both sides are lightly browned and crisp.
3. Take out and when half cold roll in caster sugar. It is best to do only 3 or 4 at a time as you need room to turn them. Any lard left over can be strained and used again.

From the Victorian recipe book of Mrs Newman

FRENCH ALMOND TART

2 discs of flaky pastry, one 10 inches in diameter, ½ inch thick, the other 8½—9 inches in diameter, ¼ inch thick

Almond paste filling
1½ oz butter
4 oz ground almonds
4 oz caster sugar
1 egg
1 tablespoon rum

Serves 6—8

1. Prepare the two discs of flaky pastry.
2. For the filling, mix the almonds and sugar, add the egg and beat.
2. Add the melted butter and rum.
4. Sandwich the discs with the filling, placing the larger disc at the bottom.
5. Glaze the top with beaten egg and bake until the pastry is cooked in a hot oven (400—425°F., Gas No. 6—7).
6. Remove from the oven and dredge with icing sugar and return to the oven for ½ minute or so.

Edward Forman

APPLE FLAPJACK PUDDING

2 oz butter or margarine   2 oz demerara sugar
3 oz oats   stewed apple

Serves 4

1. Melt butter and add the sugar.
2. Add the oats.
3. Put stewed apple in flan or pie dish and coat with the oat mixture.
4. Put it in the oven at about 375°F., Gas No. 5 for 30 minutes or until crisp and brown.

Mrs Doble

GINGER SYLLABUB

¼ *pint double cream*
1 large tablespoon advocaat
1 egg white

1 large tablespoon
ginger marmalade

Serves 2

1. Whip the cream and egg white until stiff.
2. Fold in the advocaat and ginger marmalade.
3. Spoon into glasses and serve with Boudoir fingers.

Miss M. Lovett

EVELYN'S BREAD PUDDING

1. Soak 6 oz stale bread in a basin. Break it up with a fork.
2. Add 1 beaten egg.
3. Add 1 tablespoon sugar.
4. Add 2 oz suet.
5. Add a pinch of spice.
6. If necessary moisten well with milk.
7. Add any dried fruits available to make a rich mixture.
8. Press into a pie dish. If possible arrange glacé cherries or candied peel on top.
9. Sprinkle with demerara sugar.
10. Bake until brown and set. Usually 30–40 minutes at 350°F., Gas No. 4.

Miss E. F. Dainty

ST MARTIN'S APPLE MERINGUE

½ cup demerara sugar
6 large apples
3 egg whites
   almond essence
3 teaspoons ground rice

¼ cup water
2 slices lemon peel
3 tablespoons ground almonds
3 oz caster sugar

Serves 6—8

1. Make a syrup with the sugar, water and lemon peel.
2. Peel, core and cut the apples into large cubes. Cook in the syrup until soft.
3. Remove the lemon peel and turn into a buttered oven dish. Cool.
4. Whip egg whites until stiff and gradually add the sugar.
5. Fold in the almonds, rice and almond essence.
6. Cover the apples with the mixture and bake in a moderate oven until brown.

Mrs Mary Micklewright

DEVON HONEY CRUNCH

2 tablespoons honey
½ lb crushed Nice biscuits
   whipped cream to decorate

3 oz margarine
bananas, peaches, grapes,
etc.

Serves 4—6

1. Melt the honey and margarine or butter in a saucepan over a gentle heat.
2. Add the crushed Nice biscuits and stir gently. Line a suitable dish or flan with the mixture and set aside to cool.
3. Fill the shell with fruit, sliced peaches (without their juice), or a mixture of sliced bananas and halved grapes.
4. Decorate with whipped cream. A small amount of some liqueur can be added if liked.

This is a quick and easy sweet from Devon.

Miss Hart

GLOUCESTER PUDDING

2 oz pudding rice   ½ pint milk
¼ pint water   1 small tin mandarin oranges
1 dessertspoon sugar 2 oz caster sugar
1 egg   a nut of butter

Serves 4

1. Simmer the rice, milk, water and dessertspoon of sugar in a saucepan until the rice is cooked and the mixture creamy.
2. Add the butter and some of the syrup from the oranges (remember the mixture will stiffen with baking).
3. Separate the egg, and whisk the yolk into the rice mixture.
4. Whisk the white stiffly and fold in the sugar.
5. Put the rice mixture into a pie dish, cover with the strained orange segments and spread the meringue on the top.
6. Bake in a very low oven (275°F., Gas No. 1) until the meringue is golden and crisp.
7. Serve hot.

This is most unusual and is delicious cold if you are lucky enough to have any left over!

Miss E. O'Shea

PATRICIA'S PUDDING

6 oz breadcrumbs   3 tablespoons instant coffee
3 tablespoons Cadbury's (not granules)
 drinking chocolate 3 oz dark brown sugar
½ pint double cream

Serves 4

Mix all the dry ingredients together and put in layers with the cream in between. A little rum may be added to the crumb mixture, also glacé cherries, bananas, etc., if liked.

This is best prepared several hours ahead.

Mrs R. L. Blake

BUTTERSCOTCH MERINGUE PIE

Shortcrust Pastry

6 oz self-raising flour
3 oz fat

Filling

4 oz soft brown sugar
½ pint milk
2 oz margarine

2 oz plain flour
2 egg yolks
½ teaspoon vanilla essence

Meringue
2 egg whites
4 oz caster sugar

Serves 6

1. Line shallow 8 inch pie dish with pastry and bake blind at 425°F., Gas No. 7 for 20—25 minutes.
2. Combine brown sugar and flour in saucepan. Slowly add milk and cook till thickened.
3. Cool, add egg yolks, margarine and vanilla essence. Pour in pie case.
4. Whisk egg whites until stiff. Add 2 oz caster sugar, and continue whisking until stiff. Fold in the rest of the sugar.
5. Pile meringue on top of filling, and bake at 300°F., Gas No. 2 for 20—30 minutes.

This makes a nice change from lemon meringue pie and children love it—adults too! Serve hot or cold.

Mrs Philippa Sherwin

ALMOND CHARLOTTE

4 oz ground almonds
4 oz caster sugar
    Boudoir sponge biscuits

4 oz unsalted butter
1 dessertspoon sherry

Serves 6

1. Line a 6 inch loose-bottomed cake tin with the biscuits.
2. Cream the butter, sugar and almonds together. Stir in the sherry.
3. Put in alternate layers of filling and biscuits, finishing with biscuits, and press down with a small saucer and weights.
4. Leave to mature in the fridge for 24—48 hours.

SOUFFLE OMELETTE SURPRISE

3 *standard eggs*
1 *tablespoon caster sugar*
2 *tablespoons liqueur, preferably kirsch*
1 *tablespoon caster sugar if fresh fruit is used*
1 *6—7 inch diameter thin sponge cake*

3 *tablespoons cold water*
½ *lb raspberries, sliced strawberries or mixed chopped fruits*
1 *family block vanilla ice cream*

Serves 6

1. Heat the oven to 450°F., Gas No. 8.
2. Soak the fruit in the liqueur and the sugar if required.
3. Place sponge cake on a flat oven-proof dish which is 3—4 inches wider and cover with fruit and juice.
4. Place block of ice cream, which *must* be hard, on top of this. Keep in a cool place (the ice cream must not soften).
5. Make soufflé omelette: separate eggs. Whisk yolks, water and sugar together until creamy and pale.
6. Whisk egg whites until just stiff. Fold whites into yolk mixture.
7. Then quickly cover the ice cream and sponge cake with the soufflé omelette mixture making sure that the ice cream is completely covered. You can pipe some of the omelette mixture on top as decoration. Dredge with the sugar.
8. Bake immediately in the very hot preheated oven until golden brown (about 3—5 minutes). Serve at once.

Sara Openshaw

CITRON FROMAGE

juice and rind of 2 large
lemons
5 tablespoons water
4 oz caster sugar

1 level tablespoon (1 sachet)
powdered gelatine
3 eggs
¼ pint double cream (if fresh
cream is unobtainable, bott-
led will do)

Serves 6

1. Sprinkle gelatine over 5 tablespoons water in a small pan and leave to soak for 5 minutes.
2. Separate eggs putting yolks in one large bowl and whites in another.
3. Finely grate lemon rind, mix with egg yolks and sugar and whisk until pale and creamy.
4. Squeeze lemons and strain juice into soaked gelatine. Place saucepan over low heat, stirring continuously. Do not allow to boil and immediately the gelatine has dissolved remove the pan from the heat.
5. Pour dissolved gelatine slowly into egg yolk mixture, whisking all the time. Continue to whisk until cool and the mixture begins to thicken.
6. Lightly beat cream and fold into mixture.
7. Beat egg whites until stiff and blend in evenly and lightly.
8. Spoon into a serving dish or individual dishes and chill for at least 2 hours.

Citron fromage is rich but tart.

Mrs C. Pinney

MAPLE MOUSSE

8 fl oz maple syrup
2 teaspoons gelatine dissolved
in small amount of water

2 large eggs, separated
1 teaspoon vanilla essence
1 pint whipped double cream

Serves 10

1. Boil the syrup for 2 to 3 minutes, skim if necessary.

2. Beat the yolks of the eggs, pour the hot syrup on to them slowly, stirring well.
3. Return to the saucepan and boil slowly until thickened (about the consistency of golden syrup).
4. Add the dissolved gelatine and allow to cool but not set.
5. Add the vanilla essence.
6. Fold in the whipped cream then the whisked whites of eggs.
7. Freeze.

Miss G. Murphy

STRAWBERRY ELIZABETH

1 lb strawberries, hulled and sliced, or use tinned
2 oz chopped nuts
4 oz plain flour
4 tablespoons hot water
4 oz caster sugar

½ pint double cream
4 oz butter
2 oz demerara sugar
½ oz gelatine
1 teaspoon lemon juice

a 2½ pint ring mould

Serves 6—8

1. Rub butter, demerara sugar, nuts and flour together.
2. Sprinkle in shallow baking tin and bake for 10—15 minutes at 200°F., Gas No. ¼. Leave to cool. Then crumble.
3. Soften gelatine in hot water.
4. Mash ¼ lb strawberries with lemon juice and sugar and bring to boil.
5. Add gelatine. Pour small amount into the mould through a strainer and leave to set. Allow the rest to cool.
6. Whip cream and fold in the rest of the strawberry and gelatine mixture.
7. Fill the mould with alternate layers of crumble and mixture. Chill.

Other soft fruits are equally good for this recipe, e.g. raspberries, blackberries, loganberries, etc.

Mrs Ruby Leete

6 *eggs, separated*   4 *oz caster sugar*
  grated rind and strained   ½ *oz powdered gelatine in*
  juice of 2 lemons   10 *tablespoons warm water*
  apricot jam   *whipping cream*

Serves 6–8

1. Beat the egg yolks with the caster sugar and add the grated rind and juice of 2 lemons.
2. Melt the gelatine in the water.
3. When dissolved and cool, strain this into the beaten yolks.
4. Whip the egg whites stiffly.
5. Mix lightly everything together and pour the mixture into a glass dish. When set, the bottom is very cool and lemonish and the top is delicately frothy.
6. Cover with apricot jam and whipped cream.

Mrs D. Cottam

COLD CARAMEL SOUFFLES

4 *oz sugar*   ½ *oz powdered gelatine*
  juice of 1 lemon   2 *eggs*
3 *dessertspoons sugar*   1 *egg yolk*
2 *beaten egg whites*   6 *tablespoons whipped cream*

Serves 6

1. First make the caramel. Put 4 oz sugar with ½ pint water into a small heavy pan over a low heat. Cook very slowly until the sugar has dissolved.
2. When quite melted increase the heat and cook rapidly until the syrup is very nearly golden brown.
3. Remove from the heat and stand at once on a cold surface or it will darken.
4. Add four more tablespoons of hot water, stir, and pour into a bowl to cool.
5. Dissolve gelatine in 3 tablespoons water and the lemon juice.

6. Put two eggs and one yolk into a bowl with 3 dessertspoons sugar and beat over hot water until the mixture thickens.
7. Remove, cool a little and stir in first the caramel and then the melted gelatine.
8. Stir until well blended, then leave until nearly set.
9. Fold in softly whipped cream and egg whites.
10. Turn into individual soufflé dishes to set.

Delicious on its own or to serve with summer fruit.

Mrs Ruby Leete

BROWN BREAD ICE CREAM

6 oz wholemeal breadcrumbs   *½ pint double cream*
8 oz single cream   *4 oz icing sugar*
1 tablespoon rum   *2 eggs*

Serves 4—6

1. Toast the breadcrumbs in the oven.
2. Beat the creams with sugar.
3. Mix the egg yolks with the rum and add to the creams.
4. Add the cooked breadcrumbs, whipped egg whites and freeze. No need to stir during freezing.

Mrs Felicity Savory

PINEAPPLE IGLOOS

1 pineapple slice per person
vanilla ice cream
meringue mixture as for homemade meringues

1. Place slice of pineapple on oven-proof plate.
2. Add one scoop of vanilla ice cream in centre of pineapple.
3. Pipe meringue round and over pineapple to resemble an igloo.
4. Place under the grill until brown. Serve at once.

Mrs P. Lordon

PRALINES

1 lb 4 oz granulated sugar	1 teaspoon baking soda
1 cup buttermilk	¼ teaspoon salt
3 tablespoons butter	1 lb coarsely chopped pecan nuts or walnuts

1. Using a large saucepan, mix the sugar, baking soda, buttermilk and salt and then put in a thermometer and cook over a high heat to 210°F., stirring frequently and scraping down the sides and the bottom of the saucepan.
2. Add the butter and nuts and cook, stirring continuously until the temperature reaches 230°F.
3. Remove from the heat and cool for a minute or two then beat with a wooden spoon until the mixture has thickened and has lost its gloss.
4. Immediately drop, by tablespoonfuls, on to waxed paper.

These make a very delicious pudding and can be served with cream.

John Kirkham
The Bishop of Sherborne

ICE CREAM SAUCE

2 oz dates	½ cup boiling water
1 small bottle maraschino cherries	5—6 tinned green or gold figs, chopped
2 oz flaked almonds	2 tablespoons brandy

Serves 4—6

1. Soak dates in boiling water for 3 minutes. Drain, stone and chop.
2. Add the cherries and a little of the syrup from them.
3. Add chopped figs and 2 tablespoons of their juice.
4. Toast almonds under grill.
5. Just before serving add almonds and brandy to the mixture. Stir well and spoon over plain ice cream.

Bill Sauvary

FLUMMERY DRAMBUIE

4 egg yolks
3 tablespoons drambuie
  liqueur

3 tablespoons caster sugar
7½ oz double cream

Serves 4

1. Put egg yolks and sugar in double boiler.
2. Whip quickly with beater the eggs and sugar.
3. When the mixture thickens and has increased in volume, add the drambuie.
4. Continue beating until the mixture is stiff and will stand in peaks.
5. Whip the cream until it is semi-stiff and fold it in gently.
6. Pour into individual glasses and chill.

Expensive!

Mrs J. Curtis-Brown

CARAMEL FUDGE SAUCE

1 oz sugar
1 tablespoon golden syrup
¼ pint milk
  pinch of ginger (optional)

1 tablespoon water
3 level teaspoons cornflour
2 or 3 drops vanilla essence

Serves 4

1. Put sugar and water into a saucepan and stir over low heat until sugar has dissolved.
2. Boil briskly until golden brown. Immediately stir in the golden syrup.
3. Add the blended cornflour, milk and essence and cook until well thickened.

This is very good served with baked apples, or can be stirred and thickened a little more and poured over ice cream and sprinkled with chopped walnuts.

Mrs F. Griffin

CREME A LA CREOLE

4 *bananas*
2 *oz desiccated coconut*
3 *tablespoons rum*
4 *yolks of eggs*
½ *oz gelatine*
¾ *pint milk*

3 *slices pineapple, fresh or*
  tinned
4 *oz caster sugar*
½ *pint thick cream*
1 *tablespoon brown sugar*

Serves 6

1. Slice the bananas thinly and cut the pineapple into squares.
2. Put the fruit to soak with the rum and the brown sugar turning from time to time so that it becomes well marinated.
3. Soften the gelatine in a little cold water and dissolve over hot water.
4. Beat the yolks with the sugar and the milk, and strain into a double saucepan over a low heat.
5. Stir constantly until the mixture thickens sufficiently to coat the back of a wooden spoon. It must not boil.
6. Remove from the heat and add gelatine. Stir well and strain into a large bowl. Put aside in a cool place stirring from time to time.
7. When it begins to thicken and set, slightly whip the cream and fold it into the custard mixture together with the coconut, bananas, pineapple and rum.
8. Pour into a glass dish and serve ice cold.

Mrs E. Henderson

Cakes Breads and Biscuits

BOILED FRUIT CAKE

6 oz margarine
5 oz soft brown sugar
½ level teaspoon ground cinnamon
3 oz dates
2 eggs
1 oz mixed peel
4 oz plain flour
3 oz self-raising flour

¼ pint water
¼ level teaspoon ground ginger and nutmeg
11 oz mixed sultanas, raisins and currants
2 oz glacé cherries, chopped
2 oz walnuts or almonds, chopped
½ level teaspoon bicarbonate of soda

1. Grease an 8 inch square tin, or 2 lb loaf tin and line with greaseproof paper.
2. Put the margarine in a pan with water, sugar, spices, dried fruit and dates.
3. Bring to the boil, stirring and then simmer for 3 minutes. Put aside until cold.
4. Beat the eggs and stir into the cold fruit mixture.
5. Put the chopped glacé cherries in a mixing bowl with the peel, chopped nuts and flours, sifted together with bicarbonate of soda.
6. Add the fruit mixture and stir thoroughly.
7. Put the cake mixture in a prepared tin and bake in a moderate oven (325°F., Gas No. 3) for 1½–1¾ hours. Turn out and cool on a wire rack.

This can be used as an economical Christmas cake but substitute butter for margarine, if it is to be kept for a long time.

Mrs Huss

CROSS-COUNTRY CAKE

8 oz margarine or butter
12 oz self-raising flour
½ cup of milk

8 oz demerara sugar
handful of dried fruit
1 egg

1. Melt the margarine and sugar in a large saucepan.

2. Add the flour, fruit, milk and egg and mix thoroughly.
3. Turn out on to a baking tray (as used for Swiss rolls).
4. Bake at 375°F., Gas No. 5 for about ½ hour or until brown and firm to the touch.

This cake is so called because of the vast quantities eaten by the cross-country boys after a run, it is delicious when hot, but keeps well when cut into squares and kept in a tin.

Mrs Pat Harris

SPECIAL DATE AND WALNUT CAKE

1 *breakfast cup of boiling water*
8 *oz sugar*
3 *oz butter or margarine*
1 *teaspoon vanilla essence*
½ *teaspoon salt*

8 *oz chopped dates*
1 *teaspoon bicarbonate of soda*
1 *beaten egg*
10 *oz plain flour*
1 *teaspoon baking powder*
2 *oz chopped walnuts*

Topping
5 *tablespoons brown sugar*

2 *tablespoons butter*
2 *tablespoons cream*

1. Pour the boiling water over the dates and add the bicarbonate. Allow to stand whilst the other ingredients are being mixed.
2. Mix the sugar, margarine, egg, essence, flour, baking powder, salt and walnuts together in a bowl.
3. Add the date mixture to the other ingredients, mix well and put in either 2 small well-greased and floured loaf tins or a 9 inch round tin.
4. Bake for 35 minutes in a moderate oven (350°F., Gas No.4).
5. Mix the brown sugar, butter and cream together for the topping and boil for 3 minutes.
6. Spread on the cooked and cooled cakes and sprinkle with chopped nuts (optional).

This cake is reputedly one of the Queen Mother's favourites!

Mrs Eileen Henderson

BISHOP'S CAKE (contains no fat!)

8 oz sugar
8 oz walnuts
6 oz cherries
8 oz choc. bits (or cooking
   chocolate broken into bits)
8 oz plain flour

6 oz dates
2 oz raisins (optional)
4 eggs
1½ heaped teaspoons baking
   powder
¼ teaspoon salt

1. Combine the eggs and sugar.
2. Sift the dry ingredients.
3. Add the chocolate bits, nuts and fruit.
4. Fold into the egg mixture.
5. Pour into a greased and lined 8 inch round cake tin. Bake at
   325°F., Gas No. 3 for 1½–1¾ hours.

This recipe was given by an American to a cousin of mine on a
train journey shortly after the war, when butter was scarce, and
has been a firm favourite in our family ever since.

Mrs D. Langdon

HAYMAKING CAKE

4 oz butter or margarine
2 eggs
1 lb gooseberries, washed
   and topped

4 oz caster sugar
4 oz self-raising flour

1. Cream the butter and sugar until light and fluffy.
2. Add the eggs one at a time, beating each one in thoroughly.
3. With a metal spoon carefully fold in the sifted flour.
4. Divide into 2 greased and floured sponge tins.
5. Dot the top of each with the gooseberries.
6. When cooked, turn out and whilst still warm, sandwich together with butter sprinkled with sugar.

This cake was always taken to the haymaking fields for tea.

Mrs Betty Young

DUTCH SPICY GINGER CAKE

9 oz flour
7 oz dark brown sugar
4 teaspoons baking
  powder
½ teaspoon white pepper
½ teaspoon salt
  preserved ginger or peel
  (optional)

3½ oz margarine or butter
¼ pint milk
4 teaspoons cinnamon
1 teaspoon powdered cloves
½ teaspoon nutmeg

1. Mix all the dry ingredients together.
2. Melt the butter and add this with the milk to the dry ingredients.
3. That's all! Bake for about 1½ hours at 375°F., Gas No. 5.

This cake keeps well and improves after a few days.

Mrs R. Akers

BLACKMORE VALE HUNT CAKE

¾ lb flour
¼ lb butter
1 teaspoon bicarbonate of
  soda
3 oz candied peel

¾ lb stoned raisins
¼ lb sugar
1 dessertspoon treacle
½ teacup milk

1. Cream the sugar and butter.
2. Add the flour.
3. Warm the milk and dissolve the bicarbonate and treacle.
4. Stir into the mixture and beat well.
5. Add the raisins and peel.
6. Bake for 2½ hours in a moderate oven (325°F., Gas No. 3).

I found this recipe in an old family recipe book and as I come from a Scottish hunting family, I was amused to find it north of the Border.

Mrs Norah Lisle

CARROT CAKE

2 cups plain flour	2 cups caster sugar
2 teaspoons ground cinnamon	1 teaspoon nutmeg
	2 teaspoons baking soda
1 teaspoon salt	¾ cup vegetable oil
3 large eggs	3 cups grated carrot
½ cup raisins	½ cup chopped nuts

1. Preheat oven to 350°F., Gas No. 4.
2. Grease a circular 9 inch tin with a hole in the centre.
3. Combine the flour, sugar, cinnamon, nutmeg, soda, salt and oil.
4. Beat for 2 minutes at minimum speed.
5. Add eggs one at a time. Beat well after each egg.
6. Blend in carrots, nuts and raisins.
7. Bake for 1¼ hours, cool for 5 minutes and turn out.

Can be iced with a glacé icing, this recipe is really delicious.

Mrs Carol Lea

DORSET APPLE CAKE

6 oz margarine	9 oz flour
1 dessertspoon mixed spice	1 egg
6—8 oz sugar	a little milk
4 apples	

1. Rub the margarine and flour together, mix in the sugar and spice.
2. Beat the egg and milk together and add to the mixture.
3. Peel and slice the apples into the mixture.
4. Place in a baking dish about 8x10x3 inches. Bake in a moderate oven, about 350°F., Gas No. 4 for about 1—1¼ hours. Serve hot with cream.

This is a spicy version of the Medieval Dorset recipe.

Mrs A. Vendyback

MILK CHOCOLATE CAKE

7 oz self-raising flour
8 oz caster sugar
2 tablespoons cocoa
4 oz margarine
2 eggs beaten with 5
  tablespoons evapora-
  ted milk
5 tablespoons water
1 teaspoon vanilla essence
salt

Icing
2½ oz margarine
4 tablespoons cocoa or 4 oz
  cooking chocolate
3 tablespoons milk (less if using chocolate)

1. Sift together the flour, sugar, cocoa and salt.
2. Rub in the margarine.
3. Stir in the eggs, essence, evaporated milk and water.
4. Divide into 2 deep 7 inch cake tins (*not* with loose bottoms).
5. Bake in a moderate oven 325—350°F., Gas No. 3, for approximately 35 minutes.
6. When cold sandwich together with icing, made by melting the margarine and blending in the cocoa. Stir in the milk and beat until smooth and thick.

Mrs Doreen Boyd

SCRIPTURE CAKE

2 cups 1 Kings IV 22
  (twelfth word)
2 cups 1 Samuel XXX 12
2 tablespoons Proverbs
  XXIV 13
1 pinch Leviticus 11 13
  Season with Chronicles
  2 IX 9

1 cup Judges V 25 (last clause)
1 cup Jeremiah VI 20
½ cup Numbers XVII 8
2 teaspoons Amos IV 5
½ cup Judges IV 19
3 Isaiah X 14

Cream Judges V with Jeremiah, add the rest of the ingredients. Bake 1½ hours in a moderate oven.

Mrs Mary Micklewright

Taken from a traditional Dorset recipe of the 1800s.

8 oz short crust pastry
4 large peeled and cored
apples
½ teaspoon nutmeg and
ground ginger mixed
juice of 1 lemon and 1
large slice of lemon

4 tablespoons brown breadcrumbs
4 tablespoons each of mixed
currants, chopped candied
peel, and seedless raisins
2 tablespoons sugar
2 tablespoons golden syrup

1. Cut pastry in half and roll out to fit 8 inch flan tin.
2. Lay half the pastry over the flan tin and on top put the rings of apples, overlapping.
3. Add all the other ingredients evenly and place the slice of lemon in the middle.
4. Damp the edges and cover with the remaining pastry, pressing down the edges very well. Brush with milk and bake for ½ hour in a moderate oven 350°F., Gas No. 4 until the top is golden brown.

Serve hot with cream

Matrimonial oracles are traditional to Dorset, for example, one connected with Midsummer Eve, is that a girl would put her shoes in the form of a T and say:

Hoping this night my true love to see
I place my shoes in the form of a T

Another uses an apple pip as a test of a lover's faithfulness. If it burns loudly when put on the fire, she is assured of his affection, if it burns silently, it means he is false. Whilst waiting she chants the rhyme:

If you love me pop and fly,
If you hate me, lay and die.

FRUIT MALT LOAF

2 cups All-bran
1½ cups seedless raisins
2 oz chopped walnuts
2 tablespoons black treacle

1½ cups brown sugar
4 oz chopped dates
2 cups self-raising flour
2 cups milk

1. Put all the dry ingredients in a large bowl.
2. Dissolve the treacle in the warm milk, and add to the dry ingredients. Leave to soak for one hour in the bowl.
3. Then add the flour gradually, stirring well.
4. Bake for about 1¼ hours at 325°F., Gas No. 3 in 2 greased loaf tins, lined with greaseproof paper a few inches above the tins. Turn out on to a wire tray when cool.

Mrs L. Wheadon

YUM—YUM CAKE

Cake Base
2 oz brown sugar
3 oz margarine
2 egg yolks
6 oz flour
1 teaspoon vanilla essence

Topping
2 egg whites
4 oz caster sugar
1 oz cherries
1 oz chopped walnuts

1. Cream the sugar and margarine until light and fluffy.
2. Add the egg yolks, flour and vanilla essence.
3. Mix together by hand to a stiff paste.
4. Place in a greased Swiss roll tin and flatten.
5. Whisk the egg whites until stiff.
6. Fold in the sugar, nuts and cherries.
7. Spread this evenly over the base.
8. Bake for 20—30 minutes at 350°F., Gas No. 4 or until lightly browned and the top feels crisp to the touch.

Absolutely 'yum—yum'.

Mrs K. J. James

YORKSHIRE CURD CHEESECAKE

Pastry
8 oz flour
1½ oz sugar
1 egg
4 oz butter
  pinch of salt
  milk and water

Filling
2 oz margarine

1 oz caster sugar
10 oz curd cheese
1 oz currants
1 egg
1 oz chopped peel
  lemon rind
  vanilla essence
  egg for brushing

1. Make up the pastry and line an 8 inch flan dish. Keep trimmings for decorating top.
2. Mix the margarine and sugar, add the beaten egg, cheese, peel, currants, grated lemon rind and vanilla essence.
3. Mix thoroughly and fill the prepared ring.
4. Decorate the flan with the pastry strips and brush with beaten egg.
5. Bake for 30—35 minutes at 350°F., Gas No. 4 or until lightly browned and the filling has set.

Miss Peggy Dunkley

WITWENKUSSE

4 egg whites
5½ oz ground nuts
5½ oz sugar

1. Whisk the whites of egg and the sugar in a basin over a steaming saucepan until thick.
2. Mix in the nuts.
3. Form into little rounds with 2 spoons and bake lightly in a moderate oven (300°F., Gas No. 2) for about 10 minutes.

This is an Austrian recipe, and a good way of using up whites of eggs left over from another recipe.

Mrs Margaret King

ENGERDINE NUSSTORTE

Pastry
12 oz plain flour
5 oz unsalted butter
3 oz lard
8 oz sugar
1 egg

Filling
8 oz sugar
½ pint single cream
8 oz chopped walnuts

Serves 6—8

1. Sieve the flour into a large bowl and add the sugar.
2. Rub in the butter and lard so that the mixture resembles fine breadcrumbs.
3. Bind together with a large egg.
4. Put in the fridge for about 30 minutes to chill.
5. Then grease an 8 inch loose bottomed flan tin and roll out some of the pastry to line the base of the tin, leaving sufficient for the top covering.
6. For the filling, put the sugar into a heavy-based pan and stir as it melts, immediately pour the cream into the melted sugar and add the chopped nuts.
7. Pour the mixture into the uncooked pastry case. Then roll out the remainder of the pastry and cover the top, sealing the edges.
8. Cook in a preheated oven (350°F., Gas No. 4) for approximately 35 minutes.

This is a traditional Swiss cake which improves with keeping, but must be kept in foil or in an air-tight tin, it will keep for several weeks in this way. It is rich and so only small slices are needed making it very economical!

Mrs Ursula Evans

CRUMBLE SHORTCAKE

12 oz self-raising flour
6 oz butter
   vanilla or almond essence
   (almond much the best)

5 oz granulated sugar
1 egg
6—8 oz strong jam, blackcurrant or raspberry

1. Put the butter in a saucepan and soften gently, add the other ingredients.
2. Beat the egg lightly and mix in well until it binds together evenly.
3. Put a thin layer into a well-greased sandwich tin, pressing down with your fingers.
4. Cover this with a generous layer of jam keeping it about ½ inch from the edge.
5. Then cover with the remainder of the mixture, leaving the surface rough and not pressed down.
6. Bake at medium heat (350°F., Gas No. 4) for ½—¾ hour. Test by pressing lightly in the centre and if it is firm it is cooked.

This is a very versatile recipe as it can be served hot or cold as a pudding and is delicious with cream, or cold as a cake.

Mrs Sheila Samuel

FROSTED LEMON CAKE

6 oz self-raising flour
4 oz soft margarine
4 tablespoons milk

6 oz caster sugar
2 eggs
grated rind of 1 lemon

Topping
juice of 1 lemon
6 oz caster sugar

1. Put all the ingredients in a large bowl and mix with a wooden spoon.
2. Place in a 7 inch lined cake tin.
3. Bake in a moderate oven 350°F., Gas No. 4 for 45 minutes.
4. Remove from the oven.
5. Mix the lemon juice with the caster sugar and pour evenly over the top of the cake, while the cake is still hot.
6. Leave until cold before removing from the tin.

A very successful and 'different' lemon cake.

Mrs P. J. Johnson

CHOCOLATE FUDGE CAKE

½ lb Marie biscuits
1 teacup sugar
2 tablespoons cocoa
1 teaspoon vanilla essence

1 teacup walnuts
4 oz margarine
2 eggs
lemon icing

1. Crush the biscuits lightly, leaving some pieces about the size of a 10 p. coin.
2. Chop the walnuts.
3. Melt the margarine, sugar and cocoa in a saucepan and bring to boiling point.
4. Remove the saucepan from the stove and add the eggs and vanilla essence. Beat in well.
5. Add the biscuits and walnuts and mix thoroughly.
6. Tip the contents from the saucepan into a well-buttered tin Cool in the fridge for at least 2—3 hours.
7. Remove the cake from the tin by slightly warming the outside of the tin. Turn on to a wire rack and ice the top with lemon icing.

We always served this at the New Boys Tea at Harper House and there was never any left over!

Mrs Sheila Bridge

SWISS FINGERS

4 oz butter
4 tablespoons plain flour

1 tablespoon icing sugar
few drops vanilla essence

1. Cream together butter and icing sugar, add a few drops of vanilla essence.
2. Mix in 4 tablespoons plain flour.
3. When all is smoothly blended, make into a roll and cut into 12 slices.
4. Bake in oven 350°F., Gas No. 4 for 15 minutes until pale brown.

Mrs Yates

CHOCOLATE SURPRISES

6 oz margarine
1 cup coconut
½ cup caster sugar

1 cup porridge oats
1 cup self-raising flour
3 dessertspoons drinking
chocolate

1. Melt the margarine in a saucepan.
2. Add all the other dry ingredients, and mix well.
3. Spread the mixture on a greased Swiss roll tin and bake in a moderate oven (350°F., Gas No. 4) for 25 minutes.
4. Remove from the oven and coat with chocolate icing made from 5 squares Scotbloc or 10 squares Kakebrand.
5. Leave in the tin until cold and cut into squares. Makes 24.

Mrs Anne Smart

CHOCOLATE FINGERS

4 oz margarine
2 oz caster sugar
2 teaspoons cocoa

4 oz self-raising flour
2 oz desiccated coconut

1. Cream the sugar and the margarine until light and fluffy.
2. Work in the other ingredients, no other liquid is required.
3. Spread the mixture on a greased Swiss roll tin and bake in a moderate oven (325°F., Gas No. 3) for about 25 minutes.
4. While still warm ice with chocolate icing, or melted cooking chocolate.
5. Cut into fingers when cold.

Mrs G. Abbott

MELTING MOMENTS

2½ oz lard
3 oz caster sugar
½ egg
   porridge oats

1½ oz margarine
5 oz self-raising flour
2 or 3 drops vanilla essence

1. Cream the fat and sugar until light and fluffy.
2. Beat in the egg, essence and flour.
3. Wet your hands under the cold tap and roll the mixture into little balls.
4. Put the oats in a bowl and coat the balls well.
5. Put on a greased and floured tin leaving room to spread, press out slightly with the back of a fork.
7. Cook at 375°F., Gas No. 5 for 15—20 minutes. They should be just biscuit coloured, if baked too much the oats become hard. Leave to cool slightly before removing from tin and place on a wire rack.

Miss Langdon

NEVER FAIL SWISS ROLL!

3 standard eggs
4 oz caster sugar
14x10 inch Swiss roll tin

2½ oz sifted self-raising flour
(for chocolate sponge replace
½ oz flour with ½ oz drinking chocolate)

Remember to bake sugar for 6 minutes at 425°F., Gas No. 7 otherwise the result will be *nil.*

1. Preheat oven to 425°F., Gas No. 7.
2. Cover a plate with tin foil, put the sugar on and bake for 6 minutes on one shelf above centre. Keep all the other ingredients warm.
3. Line the tin with paper oiled both sides.
4. After 6 minutes, pour the sugar on to the eggs in a warm bowl and beat with a mixer for 10 minutes or until the mixture has doubled its size.

5. Very gently fold in the flour with a spatula. Pour into the tin and smooth evenly into the corners.
6. Bake for 9 minutes one shelf above the centre at 425°F., Gas No. 7.
7. Turn out on to a floured greaseproof paper and leave to cool. Trim the edges and fill with cream and nuts or jam.
8. Roll up. You will find this easy to do without the sponge cracking.

Mrs T. J. Horsley

BUTTERSCOTCH BROWNIES

6 oz soft light brown sugar *3 oz butter*
1 egg *5 oz self-raising flour*
½ teaspoon salt *½ teaspoon vanilla essence*
2 oz shelled chopped walnuts

1. Melt the butter and the sugar together in a saucepan.
2. Stir in the beaten egg, flour, salt, vanilla essence and walnuts.
3. Spread in a greased tin approximately 7x11 inches and bake at 375°F., Gas No. 5 until set and golden.
4. Cool in tin and cut into 2 inch squares.

Mrs R. Swatridge

JUMBLES A.D. 1485

½ lb flour *½ lb sugar*
6 oz butter *1 large egg*

1. Rub flour, sugar and butter together and mix with the egg.
2. Put pieces the size of a walnut on a hot tray and cook in a medium oven (350°F., Gas No. 4) until pale brown.

This recipe is said to have been picked up on the battlefield of Bosworth, having been dropped by the cook of Richard III.

Mrs Senneck

CORNISH POTATO CAKE

1 lb self-raising flour
½ lb suet
1 oz peel
  pinch of salt

1 lb mashed potatoes
2 oz sugar
4 oz currants
  milk or buttermilk

1. Mix the ingredients to a stiff dough with some milk or buttermilk.
2. Roll out on to a greased baking sheet and bake in a hot oven until golden brown.
3. Eat hot with butter on a cold afternoon.

Mrs Joan Miller

CHOCOLATE FRUIT AND NUT CAKE

8 oz plain or milk chocolate
  digestive biscuits
2 oz packet mixed nuts
  and raisins

2 oz margarine
1 oz plain chocolate

1. Crush the biscuits.
2. Melt the margarine and chocolate in a pan over a low heat, add the nuts and raisins.
3. Stir in the digestive biscuits.
4. Spoon into a lightly greased shallow tin and press the mixture evenly.
5. Leave in a cool place to set. Cut into squares.

So easy for a child to make.

Mrs P. King

And Finally...

CRUNCHY BREAKFAST FOOD

1 lb oatmeal
2 oz sunflower seeds
2 oz sesame seeds
4 oz soft brown sugar
3 tablespoons water

1 lb wheatflakes
4 oz chopped mixed nuts
4 oz raisins
¼ pint oil

1. Mix all ingredients together in a large ovenproof pan and bake uncovered at 300°F., Gas No. 2 for 1 hour, stirring occasionally. Cool and store. Serve with milk.

Mrs Ruth Baker

ORANGE COLESLAW

1 small white cabbage
2 medium carrots
½ small onion
2 tablespoons mayonnaise
salt and pepper

2 dessert apples
2 oz raisins
1 orange yoghurt
1 dessertspoon lemon juice

1. Put the cabbage, onion, carrots, apples and raisins through the mincer, using the coarse blade.
2. Stir in the other ingredients.

Keeps very well in the fridge.

Mrs Mary Micklewright

FISHER BISCUITS

1 teacup flour
½ teacup sugar
1 large dessertspoon
   syrup

1 teacup oats
4 oz margarine
½ teaspoon baking powder
¼ teaspoon salt

1. Melt together syrup, margarine (not too hot).
2. Add sugar and stir, then add the rest of the ingredients.
3. Make into balls.
4. Cook on a greased tin for 10–15 minutes at 350°F., Gas No.5.

This biscuit recipe was always being made by a friend of mine, Mrs Fisher, the daughter-in-law of Lord Fisher, who had a large family of hungry children and as it is so easy to make has now become a great favourite in our family.

Mrs Jean Wood

CARIBBEAN CABBAGE

1 lb Dutch or firm white
   cabbage
   salt and pepper
¼ teaspoon grated nutmeg

2 large carrots
1½ oz butter or margarine
4 tablespoons water

Serves 4

1. Melt the butter in a saucepan that has a tight-fitting lid.
2. Finely shred the cabbage and carrot, add to the pan with about 4 tablespoons of water, pinch of salt and freshly ground pepper.
3. Place the lid on the pan and leave on a very low heat for 2 minutes, then stir well.
4. Check the moisture content and if necessary add a little more water.
5. Add the nutmeg and close lid and cook for about 15–20 minutes.

Serve with grilled pork chops or sausages.

Mrs Pat Weston

RUTTY'S SPECIAL (RUM PUNCH)

3 *sherry glasses of rum*
   dash of angostuara
   bitters
1 *lemon*
2 *sherry glasses of water*

2 *tablespoons grenadine syrup*
1 *tablespoon cherry brandy*
   (½ a glass together)
1 *dessertspoon sugar*

1. Cut up the lemon into little pieces.
2. Place in a liquidiser.
3. Add the sugar and the water.
4. Agitate for no more than 10 seconds.
5. Strain into a jug.
6. Add the rum, grenadine syrup, cherry brandy and bitters.
7. Place in fridge until required, or in any case for ½ hour. Serve with ice.

Alec Clifton-Taylor

FURMITY

From a letter by William Watkins, Hon. Sec. the Society of Dorset Men in London, dated Saturday 11 November 1922:

I venture to give you a recipe for the making of Furmity, which was kindly handed to me by Mrs Thomas Hardy. The recipe, I should add, is by Mrs Caddy, I know it is good:

half a pint of wheat
half a pound of raisins

half a pound of currants
two quarts of milk

Boil the wheat in water until quite tender the day before making the Furmity; boil the currants and the raisins separately.

Next day put on the milk and bring nearly to the boil, add the wheat, and let it get thoroughly cooked; then add the raisins and currants, and let it simmer for three hours or more. Add sugar (or spice if preferred), and serve in cups or basins. If it is too thick a little more milk can be added. The raisins should not be stoned, but boiled whole.

MARROW PICKLE

1. Peel the marrow, remove the seeds and pith, cut into 1 inch cubes, sprinkle with salt, cover and leave overnight.
2. Drain off the liquid the next day and to every 2 lb of marrow add:

2 oz shallots, diced
6 chillies
½ lb loaf sugar
½ oz turmeric

½ oz ground ginger
¼ oz mustard
1 quart vinegar

3. Put the vinegar in the pan to boil with the marrow, shallots, chillies, sugar and ginger.
4. Save a few tablespoons of vinegar and mix with the turmeric and mustard, then add slowly to the boiling marrow.
5. Allow to simmer for about 20 minutes or until thick, cool and pot up as for jam.

Lady Boyd

A DIFFERENT WAY WITH BEETROOT

1 lb beetroot, cooked,
*   peeled and diced*
6 tablespoons vinegar
1 tablespoon flour
stock or water

½ lb onions, peeled and
*   chopped*
2 tablespoons brown sugar
pepper and salt

1. Fry the onions until golden brown.
2. Add a good tablespoon of flour to onions and fat in the pan and work up to a paste. Fry for a minute, stirring all the time.
3. Add enough stock or water to bring to a pouring consistency, then add diced beetroot.
4. Cook for about 5 minutes, then add 2 good tablespoons of sugar and about 6 tablespoons of vinegar. Season well with salt and pepper. Correct seasoning by adding more sugar or vinegar to taste.

Mrs Betty Brook

RHUBARB CHUTNEY

1½ pints wine vinegar
4 onions
1 lb demerara sugar
3 oz salt
cayenne pepper

4 lb rhubarb
1 lb stoned dates
¼ lb sultanas
½ oz garlic (optional)
½ oz chillies

1. Chop the rhubarb into small pieces.
2. Finely slice the onions.
3. Chop the dates.
4. Place all the ingredients in a saucepan with the wine vinegar.
5. Bring to the boil and then simmer until tender.
6. When cool, jar as usual.

Mrs Jean Cornell

JULIENNE OF CELERY AND POTATOES

1 shallot, chopped
1 head celery

2—3 potatoes
1 oz butter

1. Cut the potato and celery into julienne strips.
2. Heat the butter in a sauté pan and add the shallots and shake over the heat for 4—5 minutes.
3. Then add the celery, cook a little, add potatoes, season, cover with buttered paper and a lid and continue to cook on the stove top or in the oven until the vegetables are tender.

This is a very good accompaniment to pheasant.

Mrs Grazebrook

3 *lb wholemeal flour*	1 *dessertspoon dried yeast*
1 *level dessertspoon salt*	1 *heaped dessertspoon dark*
2 *pints warm water*	*brown sugar*

1. Soak the yeast in a little water until reconstituted.
2. Grease and flour three 1 lb bread tins.
3. To the yeast add the sugar, flour and lastly salt; pour in about 1½ pints warm water, mix with hand, then leave for an hour or longer.
4. Knead for a few minutes more, divide and put into tins to rise until well up in tins, for about 30–40 minutes.
5. Bake for about ½ hour in oven preheated to 400°F., Gas No. 6.
6. Take the bread out of the tins and replace upside down in oven for about 10 minutes until it makes a hollow sound when tapped.
7. Cool on rack.

I started making brown bread some 17 years ago—convinced that the nutritional value of wholemeal flour was far greater than other flours. The recipe I have put forward here was written in response to the need at the Natural Resources Development College, Lusaka, Zambia. While we were in Africa I realised that more and more Africans were turning to the inadequate Europeans' diet and white bread. I was fortunate in being given time on Kenyan and Zambian television to demonstrate bread-making and to explain the nutritional qualities of brown bread.

Mrs M. Good

POT POURRI A LA SARAH, DUCHESS OF MARLBOROUGH
Seventeenth—eighteenth century

'Lavender, marjoram, rosemary, thyme, bay leaves, orange leaves, damask roses, blown buds of violets, jessamin (jasmin), mock orange and orange blossom all picked from the green excepting the orange flowers.

1 oz orrice root powdered
1 oz Benjamin storax
½ oz musk
2 lb bay salt
   dried orange stuck with cloves
   put in 1 oz of bruised cloves
      1 oz nutmeg grated find to raise the smell

Take a jar that shuts close. Lay a layer of blossoms and a layer of spices alternately until all is in. Let it stand a fortnight and then stir every day for a month. Let it stand in the sun.'

I have never yet managed to find all the ingredients and Benjamin storax has baffled me, but even without some of the ingredients this is an excellent basis for a good pot pourri.

Mrs Frances Moule

SLOE GIN

12 oz ripe sloes
½ bottle gin
10 oz candy or brown crystal coffee sugar

1. Prick the fruit and place in a jar with the sugar and cover with gin.
2. Stir occasionally with a wooden spoon. Leave for 3 months.
3. Strain and bottle.

Mrs F. Whitehouse

EASTER CAKES

1 lb self-raising flour
½ lb caster sugar
   a little nutmeg
   brandy or lemon flav-
   ouring

½ lb butter
2 oz washed and dried currants
2 eggs and 2 yolks

1. Mix the flour, butter and caster sugar.
2. Add the other ingredients, take care not to make it too wet with the egg yolks.
3. Roll out, cut with your usual biscuit cutter, and bake for about 10—15 minutes in a hot oven, 425°F., Gas No. 7.
4. Turn out on to a wire rack and dust with caster sugar.

Mrs V. English

ALWESTON WHIRLS

8 oz puff, rough puff or   4 oz streaky bacon, chopped
  flaky pastry   3—4 oz grated cheese
  Marmite

Serves 4—6

1. Roll the pastry out into a rectangle, trim the edges if necessary.
2. Spread thinly with Marmite.
3. Sprinkle with chopped bacon and grated cheese.
4. Roll up the pastry like a Swiss roll, starting from a long side.
5. Cut roll into ½ inch thick slices and place on a baking tray.
6. Bake for 15—20 minutes at 425°F., Gas No. 7 until golden brown.

Mrs J. Bush

IAIN'S OATMEAL STUFFING

1 cup coarse oatmeal   3 oz butter
1 onion, chopped fine   1 apple, chopped fine
  salt and pepper to taste   1 teaspoon dry mustard
1 dessertspoon lemon   1 saltspoon sugar
  juice

1. Toast oatmeal under grill or in oven.
2. Fry onion and apple in butter.
3. Add seasoning and oatmeal.
4. Add lemon and sugar and herbs if liked.
5. Mix into a stiff paste and fill chicken or any other bird.

Iain Stuart Robertson

CONVERSION TABLE

With the change to metric measures many readers will be using kitchen equipment marked in metric quantities. There is no need to throw away recipes or do lengthy calculations to convert ounces to grams or pints to litres. The following convertion charts are based on the advice given by the Metrication Board in the leaflets they prepared during the change-over period.

Although to make conversion simpler, the advised weight unit of 25 grams is slightly smaller than an ounce and the liquid unit of ½ litre is slightly less than a pint, the proportion of 25 g solid to 500 ml is the same proportion as 1 oz to 1 pint, so your recipes will be just as reliable using the following charts:

WEIGHT

oz	1	2	3	4	6	8	10	12	14
g	25	50	75	100	150	200	250	300	350

lb	1	2	3	4	5	6	7	8
kg	½	1	1½	2	2½	3	3½	4

LIQUID MEASURE

pints	1/8	¼	½	¾	1	1½	2
ml	62	125	250	375	500	750	1000

pints	2	3	4	5	6	7	8
litres	1	1½	2	2½	3	3½	4

INDEX